A SAINSBURY COOKBOOK

THE COOKING OF
BURGUNDY
AND THE LYONNAIS

ANNE WILLAN

CONTENTS

Published exclusively for J Sainsbury plc
Stamford House   Stamford Street
London SE1 9LL
by Martin Books,
Simon & Schuster Consumer Group
Grafton House   64 Maids Causeway
Cambridge CB5 8DD

ISBN 0 85941 488 4

First published 1987
Second impression October 1992
Text, photographs and illustrations
© J Sainsbury plc 1987

Printed in Italy by Printer Trento

THE AUTHOR

Anne Willan was born in Yorkshire. After reading economics at Cambridge, she studied and taught cooking in London and Paris. From there she moved to the United States, where she worked on *Gourmet* magazine and was food editor of the *Washington Star*, as well as editing the 20-volume *Grand Diplôme Cooking Course*.

She is best-known in Britain as founder and President of l'École de Cuisine La Varenne in Paris and the author of cookery books such as *The Observer French Cookery School* and the award-winning *French Regional Cooking*.

Anne now lives in Washington DC with her husband Mark Cherniavsky, an international economist. They also have a home in Burgundy, where they spend some time each year.

INTRODUCTION

So many good things grow in Burgundy! Our garden overlooking the river Yonne overflows with berries, salad greens, beans, fresh herbs and all the members of the onion family including garlic. The local market stalls offer farm-raised poultry and the best selection of cheeses I've seen outside a major city. Burgundian beef from the famous Charollais cattle is renowned far outside France and as for the Lyonnais hams and sausages, I could survive on them alone without a moment's regret.

For the traveller, Burgundy is best known as the road south from Paris which was made agreeable, until the era of autoroutes, by some of the finest inns in Europe. Burgundy and the neighbouring Lyonnais offer much much more, however, from the foothills of the Alps in the south east, home of the chickens of Bresse, to the cattle country of Nièvre at the western extremity. In the centre rise the mountains of the Morvan national park, while Dijon, Lyon, and the wine towns of the Côte d'Or – the slope of gold –

exhude an air of confidence. Wealth gleams everywhere – the wealth of vineyards and of some of the finest agricultural land in France – and goes back so many centuries that the province is littered with splendid abbeys and châteaux.

The Burgundian tradition of hospitality had already begun in the fifteenth century, when the Duchy stretched from Flanders to south of Lyon. The ducal palace of Dijon boasts an octagonal kitchen with four stone fireplaces leading to a single chimney. 'Some have built a hearth in their kitchen,' exclaimed Curnonsky, the self-styled Prince of Gastronomes, 'but the Dukes of Burgundy, they have made a kitchen from their hearth!' Good eating continues at the feasts still held at the end of the wine harvest and at the banquets of the gastronomic societies like the *Commanderie des Cordons Bleus*.

But the very best Burgundian food is enjoyed at home. The respect given to the women chefs of Lyon – the *mères* – is no coincidence, for they cook with a warmth and generosity that reflects the spirit of the region. I once toured the Lyon market with Léa, a cook of the old school with a

5

bistro on the banks of the river Saône. She cleared the way with a bullhorn, joshing the stallholders with an easy camaraderie that was amply returned.

Identifying the dishes of Burgundy and the Lyonnais is surprisingly difficult, for many are so simple as to require no recipe at all. The novelist Colette, who was brought up in the Puisaye, just east of Auxerre, talks of the 'primitive, almost brutal gourmandise' of the chicken roasted and glazed over coals. One unifying element is wine, which is not unexpected for all over the world the best cooks always go for home-grown ingredients. Yet somehow no other region goes to quite the same lengths as Burgundy, which even adapts red wine to fish and eggs in red wine *meurette* sauce. White wine is a staple ingredient in parsleyed ham in aspic, *pochouse* fish stew, a dozen meat and poultry dishes and of course the famous snails *bourguignonne*.

To me, Burgundian cooking is country cooking and I've been lucky enough to have two outstanding teachers: Chef Chambrette from École de Cuisine La Varenne in Paris and Madame Milbert, the caretaker's wife who picks the vegetables and raises the rabbits. It was Madame Milbert who told me to cook kidney beans with red wine and savory and it was she who introduced me to home-brewed *cassis*, or blackcurrant liqueur, and her husband's fiery Calvados. As for Chef Chambrette, veteran of 50 years behind the stove, his instinctive understanding of ingredients is an education. As he surveys the table before class, I feel he looks each fish in the eye with a telepathic message.

This is a very personal book: a collection of recipes that reflect our family life in summer in the northern tip of Burgundy, near Sens. Our house looks out over the Yonne river to the cornfields. The wine press still stands in the barn and the bread oven is in working order. The Burgundian tradition of hospitality seems very much alive and I hope I can pass on just a little of its magic.

Note on recipes

All recipes in this book give ingredients in both metric (g, ml, etc.) and imperial (oz, pints, etc.) measures. Use either set of quantities, but not both, in any one recipe. All teaspoons and table-spoons are level unless otherwise stated. Egg size is medium (size 3) unless otherwise stated. Preparation and cooking times are given as a guideline: all timings are approximate.

BASIC METHODS

These form part of several recipes in this book. Each recipe gives specific quantities which you should use and refers you to the method described here.

CRÈME FRAÎCHE

Most French cream has a slightly tart flavour which is particularly good in sauces.

To make *crème fraîche*, stir together in a saucepan twice as much double cream as buttermilk or soured cream. Heat gently until just below body temperature, 25°C/75°F. Pour the cream into a container and partly cover it. Keep it at this temperature for 6–8 hours or until it has thickened and tastes slightly acid. The cream will thicken faster on a hot day. Stir it and store it in the refrigerator; it will keep for up to two weeks.

CROÛTES

Croûtes are fried slices of bread used to add texture and substance as well as to garnish dishes. When using french bread, cut the loaf in thin, diagonal slices; when using sliced white bread, cut the bread into triangles, circles, hearts or tear-drop shapes, discarding crusts.

To fry croûtes: heat enough oil or butter, or a mixture of the two, to coat the base of a frying pan generously. When the fat is very hot, add a layer of croûtes, brown them on both sides over a brisk heat and drain them on paper towels. Croûtes can be made ahead, stored in an airtight jar and reheated in a low oven.

CROÛTONS

Croûtons are small croûtes made of sliced white bread, cut in dice with crusts removed. In a frying pan, heat enough oil or butter, or a mixture of the two, for the croûtons to float. When the fat is very hot, add the diced bread and fry it briskly, stirring constantly so they brown evenly. Lift them out with a draining spoon and drain on paper towels. Croûtons can be stored in an airtight jar and reheated in a low oven.

FISH STOCK

Fish stock is made from the uncooked bones and heads of fish. Often these are left after filleting, but if the fish is to be cooked whole, extra bones will be needed. To make fish stock: break the bones into pieces and rinse them under cold water. Put them in a pan with onion, bouquet garni, peppercorns, wine and water. Bring to the boil and skim. Lower the heat, simmer uncovered for 20 minutes and strain. Fish stock can be kept for up to two days in the refrigerator, or frozen for up to three months.

BEURRE MANIÉ (KNEADED BUTTER)

Kneaded butter is a mixture of butter and flour used to thicken a liquid at the end of cooking. It gives a richer, more traditional sauce than one thickened with arrowroot or cornflour. To make it, work equal quantities of butter and flour together with a fork until smooth. Add the kneaded butter to boiling liquid, whisking constantly so the butter melts and distributes the flour, thus thickening the sauce evenly. The butter should be added piece by piece until the sauce has thickened to the consistency you want. *Beurre manié* can be made in large quantities and kept for several weeks in the refrigerator.

PÂTE BRISÉE

French *pâte brisée* is used for both savoury and sweet turnovers, pies and tarts. The dough is made pliable by kneading on the work surface and it should always be thinly rolled. Suitable quantities of ingredients are given in each recipe which calls for *pâte brisée*.

To make it, sift the flour on to a work surface and make a large well in the centre. Pound the butter with a rolling pin to soften it. Put the butter, egg yolks or eggs, salt and most of the water in the well with flavourings such as sugar. Work these ingredients together with the fingertips of one hand until they are partly mixed. Gradually draw in the flour, pulling the dough into large crumbs using the fingertips of both hands. If the crumbs are dry, sprinkle on more water. Press the dough together; it should be soft but not sticky.

Work the dough with the heel of your hand, pushing it away from you on the work surface and then gathering it up with a spatula; continue for 1–2 minutes until the dough is smooth and pliable. Press it into a ball, wrap and chill it for 30 minutes or until firm. *Pâte brisée* dough can be kept overnight in the refrigerator, or frozen.

VINAIGRETTE DRESSING

Vinaigrette dressing can be made with neutral salad oil, olive oil or a nut oil. In France, wine vinegar is usually used in vinaigrette, in the proportion of three of oil to one of vinegar, but about half the amount of lemon juice can be substituted for the vinegar. Flavourings such as chopped shallot or herbs should be added to the dressing just before you use it.

To make vinaigrette, whisk the vinegar with a little salt, pepper and mustard. Gradually whisk in the oil so the dressing thickens slightly. Season it to taste with salt and pepper. The dressing will separate on standing but can be re-emulsified by whisking.

HORS D'OEUVRE AND SOUPS

First courses are a serious matter in Burgundy. Snails, nine or a dozen of them, are one of the lighter alternatives to eggs in red wine sauce, or a fish stew. Soups are hearty, based on vegetables and fortified with bread croûtes. Onion soup was listed by Rabelais as one of the typical *soupes lionnaises* during a stay in Lyon in the early 1500s.

LA GRATINÉE LYONNAISE

Lyonnais onion soup   Serves 4

Preparation time: 10 minutes + 1 hour 20 minutes cooking

50 g (2 oz) unsalted butter, plus extra for greasing

1 kg (2 lb) yellow onions, sliced thinly

1.25 litres (2¼ pints) veal or beef stock

1 bay leaf

8–12 fried bread croûtes, made with french bread (page 7)

150 g (5 oz) Gruyère cheese, grated

salt and pepper

When making onion soup, much the most important point is to use tart yellow onions, browning them so thoroughly in butter that they caramelise and give a characteristic toasted flavour. If you have no home-made stock, use canned consommé rather than a bouillon cube.

Melt the butter in a heavy-based pan. Add the sliced onions, salt and pepper and press a piece of buttered foil on top. Cover and cook gently, stirring occasionally, until the onions are very soft, 25–30 minutes. Remove the foil and continue cooking them on a medium heat for another 15–20 minutes until golden, stirring so they do not burn.

Add the stock and bay leaf and simmer for 20–30 minutes. Discard the bay leaf and season the soup to taste. It can be stored for up to three days in the refrigerator.

To finish: preheat the grill and bring the soup to the boil. Put 2–3 croûtes in each of four heatproof bowls, pour over the soup and sprinkle it generously with the grated cheese. Grill until the cheese is bubbly and browned. Serve the soup at once, while scalding hot.

GÂTEAU DE FOIES DE VOLAILLE, COULIS DE TOMATE AUX HERBES

Hot chicken liver mousse with fresh tomato and herb sauce   Serves 6

Preparation time: 50 minutes + 25 minutes cooking

vegetable oil for greasing

225 g (7 oz) carton of chicken livers, cut in pieces

1 clove of garlic, peeled

30 g (1¼ oz) plain flour

4 eggs, beaten to mix

4 egg yolks

4 tablespoons crème fraîche (page 7) or double cream

375 ml (13 fl oz) milk

a pinch of grated nutmeg

For the tomato coulis:

750 g (1½ lb) tomatoes, peeled, de-seeded and chopped finely

3 tablespoons chopped fresh herbs such as chives, basil, oregano or parsley

juice of ½ lemon

salt and pepper

To garnish:

6 stems of chive or sprigs of basil, oregano or parsley

Oven temperature:
Gas Mark 3/170°C/325°F

A hot liver mousse might seem to have limited appeal, yet every time we make this classic Burgundian dish in cooking classes it is a resounding success. Around Bresse, where the mousse originates, it is served with a crayfish or prawn sauce, like the one in Quenelles aux Crevettes (Fish dumplings with prawn sauce, page 41), but when tomatoes are in season I much prefer this fresh tomato 'coulis' flavoured with basil, chives, oregano or parsley. This dish is cooked in a water bath, because it needs a consistently low heat so that the mousses cook to the centre without overcooking on the outside, and remain moist.

Brush six 125 ml (4 fl oz) ramekins with oil and line them with rounds of greaseproof or waxed paper. Preheat the oven.

Purée the chicken livers with the garlic in a food processor or blender and pour the purée into a bowl. Beat in the flour and then the eggs, egg yolks, *crème fraîche* or cream, milk, nutmeg, salt and pepper. Fry a teaspoonful of the mixture in a frying pan and then taste it for seasoning; it should be delicate but not bland. Work the mixture through a sieve and then pour it into the ramekins. The mixture rises in the oven, so don't fill them more than three-quarters full.

Fill a large shallow pan such as a roasting tin with hot water to within 2.5 cm (1 inch) of the top. Set the ramekins in the water bath and bring it to the boil on top of the stove. Then transfer it to the oven and bake until the mousses are firm and a skewer inserted in the centre comes out clean, 20–25 minutes. The cooked mousses can be stored in the refrigerator for up to two days.

For the *coulis:* put the chopped tomatoes in a sieve and lightly season them with salt and pepper. Leave them for 30 minutes to drain off any excess liquid. Mix the tomatoes in a bowl with the chopped herbs and season them to taste with lemon juice, salt and pepper. The *coulis* can be kept for 2–3 hours at room temperature but do not chill it.

Shortly before serving, reheat the mousses in a water bath on top of the stove for 10–15 minutes, if necessary. Unmould them on to individual plates and spoon the *coulis* around the edge. Decorate each mousse with a sprig of herb and serve at once.

ESCARGOTS AU BEURRE D'ANCHOIS

Snails in anchovy butter   Serves 6

Preparation and cooking time: 20 minutes

54 *large canned snails*

250 g (8 oz) *unsalted butter, softened*

3 *tablespoons white wine*

4–5 *anchovy fillets, chopped finely*

1 *shallot, chopped finely*

3 *cloves of garlic, or more to taste, chopped finely*

3 *tablespoons finely chopped parsley*

salt and pepper

Oven temperature (optional):
Gas Mark 9/250°C/475°F

A book on the cooking of Burgundy must surely have a recipe for snails! Prized by the Romans, the big white 'escargot de Bourgogne' still exists in profusion, ready for gathering after any shower of rain. Preparing them, however, is a week-long operation of purging, cleaning, simmering and shelling before cooking even begins. Much more practical is to buy prepared snails which come from specialised French farms where literally millions are canned or frozen every week.

Drain the snails, rinse them and divide them among six ceramic snail dishes or ramekins. For the anchovy butter, first beat the unsalted butter until it is very soft. Stir in the wine, anchovies, shallot, garlic and parsley. Season to taste with salt and pepper, but if the anchovies are very salty, more salt may not be needed. Spoon the anchovy butter over the snails. All this preparation can be done up to 24 hours ahead and the snails kept in the refrigerator.

To finish, first preheat the grill or oven. Grill the snails for about 5 minutes or bake them in the oven for about 7 minutes, until very hot and lightly browned. Serve at once with plenty of french bread.

Escargots au Beurre d'Anchois
Gâteau de Foies de Volaille, Coulis de Tomate aux Herbes

FONDS D'ARTICHAUTS À LA MOUSSE DE FOIE GRAS

Artichoke bottoms with *foie gras* mousse   Serves 10

Preparation and cooking time: 1¼ hours

1 lemon

10 globe artichokes

180 g (6 oz) can of pâté de
foie gras or good liver pâté

125 g (4 oz) unsalted
butter, softened

1–2 tablespoons cognac

175 ml (6 fl oz) crème
fraîche (page 7) or double
cream

vinaigrette dressing made
with 2 tablespoons wine
vinegar, ½ teaspoon Dijon
mustard and 6 tablespoons
oil (page 9)

salt and pepper

To garnish:

1 small canned truffle or
10 black olives

*A favourite occupation for idle students in cooking
class is the preparation of artichoke bottoms. It's true
they take time, but the results are delicious enough to
merit the filling of foie gras I enjoyed last time I
lunched at Tournus, opposite the famous romanesque
abbey. You can always resort to time-saving artichoke
bottoms in cans.*

To prepare the artichokes: add the juice of half
the lemon to a bowl of cold water. Break the
stems from the artichokes so any fibres are pulled
from the flesh. With a very sharp knife held
against the side of the artichoke, cut off all the
large bottom leaves, leaving a soft cone of central
leaves. Trim the cone level with the top of the
artichoke base and rub the base well with the cut
lemon to stop it discolouring. Cut off the leaves
under the base, turning as if peeling an apple,
and trim it smooth, flattening the bottom so it
sits firmly. Rub again with a cut lemon and soak
in cold water.

To cook the artichokes: bring a large pan of
salted water to the boil. Drain the artichokes,
put them in the boiling water and cover with a
heatproof plate so they do not float. Simmer
them for 15–20 minutes or until they are tender.
Drain them, let them cool slightly and then
scoop out the choke with a teaspoon.

For the mousse: work the pâté through a sieve
with the butter and beat them until they are soft
and creamy. If you are using a truffle to garnish,
reserve the juice, trim the truffle and cut it in ten
slices. Chop the trimmings and stir them with
the juice into the pâté mixture, with the cognac.
Whip the *crème fraîche* or cream until it has
slightly thickened and stir it into the pâté as well.
Take care not to over-mix or the cream will
separate. Season the mousse to taste with salt

and pepper. The artichokes and mousse can be kept in the refrigerator for up to 24 hours.

To finish: dip the artichoke bottoms in vinaigrette dressing and set them on individual plates. Using a pastry bag and large star tube, pipe large rosettes of mousse into the artichokes, or fill them using two spoons. Top with a slice of truffle or an olive and serve at room temperature.

TARTE AUX EPINARDS ET À L'OSEILLE

Sorrel and spinach tart
Serves 8

Preparation time: 40 minutes + 25 minutes cooking

pâte brisée made with 200 g (7 oz) flour, 85 g (3½ oz) unsalted butter, 1 egg yolk, ½ teaspoon salt and 2 tablespoons or more cold water (page 8)

For the filling:

350 g (12 oz) fresh or frozen and thawed leaf spinach

25 g (1 oz) unsalted butter, plus extra for greasing

500 g (1 lb) fresh sorrel

250 ml (8 fl oz) crème fraîche (page 7) or double cream

2 egg yolks

grated nutmeg

50 g (2 oz) Gruyère cheese, grated

salt and pepper

Oven temperatures:
Gas Mark 6/200°C/400°F
Gas Mark 4/180°C/350°F

Sorrel grows like a weed in the garden and the supply of it always seems to outstrip demand, as not everyone likes its acid taste. In this recipe, spinach acts as a balance and can replace the sorrel altogether if you prefer.

Lightly butter a 25 cm (10-inch) tart tin. Roll out the *pâte brisée* dough about 5 cm (2 inches) larger than the tin. Roll the dough around the rolling pin and then unroll it over the tin, being careful not to stretch it. Gently lift the edges and press the dough well into the corners using a small ball of dough dipped in flour. With your fingers, press the dough evenly up the edge of the tin to increase the height of the shell. Prick the dough all over with a fork and chill it for 15 minutes or until firm. Preheat the oven to the higher setting.

Line the chilled pastry shell with greaseproof paper, pressing it well into the corners; fill the tin with dried beans or rice. Bake the shell in the oven for 15 minutes or until the pastry edges are set and lightly browned. Remove the paper and continue baking for 5 minutes and then let it cool. Lower the oven heat to the second setting.

Tear the stems from the spinach, wash the leaves thoroughly in several changes of cold water and drain them. Pack the spinach in a saucepan, add 1.5 cm (½-inch) water and cover. Cook over a medium heat, stirring occasionally, for about 5 minutes or until the spinach is wilted and just tender. Drain it in a colander, rinse it with cold water and drain again. Press the spinach in your fists to extract all the water. Melt half the butter in the pan, add the spinach and cook it gently, stirring, until the spinach is very dry. Let it cool and then chop it coarsely. Prepare and cook frozen spinach as directed on the packet.

Discard the stems from the sorrel and wash it thoroughly in 2–3 changes of water. Melt the remaining butter in a pan, add the sorrel and cook it for about 5 minutes, stirring constantly until it softens into a purée and the liquid evaporates. Let it cool also.

Stir the spinach into the sorrel, followed by the *crème fraîche* or cream and the egg yolks. Season the mixture to taste with nutmeg, salt and pepper and pour it into the tart shell. Sprinkle the top of the tart with cheese and bake it in the oven until puffed and browned, 25–30 minutes. Serve the tart hot or at room temperature. It is best eaten the day it is baked, but can be kept for a day in the refrigerator.

PETITS OREILLERS DE LA BELLE AURORE

Little pillows with turkey and currants   Serves 4–6

Preparation time: 1 hour + 30 minutes chilling + 20 minutes cooking

40 g (1½ oz) currants

175 g (6 oz) cooked turkey, without skin or bone

1 onion, chopped finely

25 g (1 oz) unsalted butter

3 tablespoons chopped chives, tarragon or parsley

2 tablespoons fresh breadcrumbs

1–2 tablespoons double cream

pâte brisée made with 250 g (8 oz) plain flour, 125 g (4 oz) unsalted butter, 1 egg,

In the early nineteenth century, gastronome Brillat-Savarin named this legendary recipe after his mother, Aurore, who was a native of Belley, near Nantua, and therefore almost a Burgundian. In his day the pastry 'pillow' overflowed with a mixture of partridge, veal, pork, duck, chicken, hare, beef, marrow, truffles and pistachios. The following more manageable version, stuffed with currants and the remains of the Christmas turkey, appeared on the table of a friend of mine with a taste for whimsical names. The little pillows can be deep-fried or baked in the oven.

For the filling, pour boiling water over the currants, leave them to soak for 5 minutes and

Petits Oreillers de la Belle Aurore

1 teaspoon salt and 3–4 tablespoons cold water (page 8)

1 egg, beaten lightly with ½ teaspoon salt

vegetable oil for deep-frying (optional)

salt and pepper

Oven temperature (optional):
Gas Mark 5/190°C/375°F

·drain them. Work the turkey through the fine blade of a mincer or finely chop it. Fry the onion in the butter until it is soft but not browned and mix it into the turkey with the currants, herbs, breadcrumbs, cream and salt and pepper to taste.

Divide the pastry dough in half and roll each to a 35 cm (14-inch) square, trimming the edges. Brush one square with egg glaze and spoon the filling in 16 mounds on the dough, as for ravioli. Roll the second square of dough around the rolling pin and unroll it to cover the filling. With your fingers, press around each mound of filling to seal it in. Using a knife or a fluted ravioli or pastry wheel cutter, cut between the mounds. Roll out any remaining dough and make additional 'pillows'. Chill the 'pillows' for 30 minutes or until firm.

If you are baking the 'pillows', preheat the oven. Brush them with egg glaze, set them on a baking sheet and bake for 15–20 minutes until they are crisp and browned. They can be stored for up to two days in an airtight container and reheated in a low oven just before serving.

If you are deep-frying the 'pillows', heat the oil to 190°C/375°F and fry a few 'pillows' at a time until golden brown. Drain them on paper towels and keep them warm in a low oven with the door open while you fry the rest. Serve them at once.

CHARCUTERIE

Charcuterie and anything to do with the pig are far and away the most popular start to a Burgundian meal. Sausages dominate; dried or smoked, skinny or plump, coarse-cut or smooth. Lyon has its *rosette*, dry-cured and dark, studded with nuggets of fat. The smoked hams of the Morvan hills just west of the Côte d'Or are the equal of any from Italy. As for pâtés and terrines, I look for old-fashioned mixtures with rabbit and pork, or the parsleyed ham, set with shallots in a wine aspic, that glows like a jewel on the charcutier's counter.

SAUCISSON À L'AIL AUX NOISETTES

Garlic sausage with hazelnuts   Serves 8

Preparation time: 15 minutes + chilling overnight + 1 hour cooking

40 cm (16 inches) of large sausage casing (optional)
4–5 cloves of garlic, chopped finely
25 g (1 oz) unsalted butter
750 g (1½ lb) lean pork
250 g (8 oz) pork fat
2½ teaspoons salt
white pepper
grated nutmeg
2 tablespoons brandy or Madeira
50 g (2 oz) hazelnuts, toasted

A speciality of Lyon, this fresh garlic sausage is poached in water before being sliced to serve warm with potato vinaigrette or being baked in brioche dough as in the recipe on page 20. Pistachios are usually added for their colour, but I once substituted toasted hazelnuts and have done so ever since. If you cannot find sausage casings, the stuffing can also be shaped using greaseproof paper and muslin.

Soak the casing in cold running water for 5–10 minutes and then attach it to the tap and run water through to rinse it. Cook the garlic in the butter for 1–2 minutes until it is soft but do not brown it.

Work the lean pork and pork fat through the fine blade of a mincer. Put them in a bowl with the garlic, salt, pepper, nutmeg and brandy or Madeira and beat well to mix in the seasonings. Rub the hazelnuts in a rough towel while they are still very hot, to remove the skins. Chop them and stir them into the mixture. Fry a small piece of mixture and taste it: it should be highly seasoned, so add more seasoning if necessary.

Attach one end of the casing to a sausage stuffer or wide-based funnel and knot the other end. Push the meat mixture through and into the casing, easing it down towards the tied end. Shape it into a compact sausage about 40 cm (16 inches) long; do not pack it too tightly or it will burst during cooking. Twist the centre to divide the sausage in two and knot the other end. Prick any air bubbles with a pin. Refrigerate the sausage overnight, or for up to 24 hours.

To poach the sausage, first prick it several times. Put it in cold water to cover and heat to just below boiling point; if the water boils, the sausage will burst. Poach it for ¾–1 hour until a skewer becomes hot after being pushed into the centre. For serving, discard the casing and cut the sausage in fairly thin slices.

To cook the sausage without a casing, butter two 20 cm (8-inch) square sheets of greaseproof paper. Divide the sausage mixture in half, spread it across the centre of each of the papers to form neat cylinders and then roll up the paper. Wrap the cylinders tightly in muslin, tying the ends. Poach the sausages in the same way as if they were cased.

SAUCISSON EN BRIOCHE

Garlic sausage in brioche   Serves 8–10

Preparation time: 35 minutes + 3 hours rising + 6 hours chilling + 45 minutes baking + 1¼ hours and chilling overnight to make the sausage

15 g (½ oz) dried yeast
4 tablespoons lukewarm water
500 g (1 lb) plain flour, or more if needed
2 teaspoons salt
1 tablespoon caster sugar
6 eggs, beaten
oil for greasing

This quick brioche dough was taught to me by a Frenchwoman who habitually entertained upwards of twenty members of her family. With no time to spare she relied on half a dozen foolproof specialities and this was one of them. To speed things up, I often make the dough in an electric mixer with only a nostalgic thought about kneading by hand, which is one of the most satisfying but tiring of all culinary occupations.

Sprinkle the yeast over the water in a small bowl and leave it for about 5 minutes until dissolved. Sift the flour into the mixer bowl, adding the salt

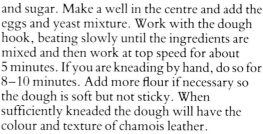

250 g (8 oz) unsalted butter, cut in pieces, plus extra for greasing

2 × 500 g (1 lb) saucissons a l'ail aux noisettes (garlic sausages with hazelnuts, page 19), poached and chilled

1 egg, beaten with ½ teaspoon salt

Oven temperature:
Gas Mark 6/200°C/400°F

and sugar. Make a well in the centre and add the eggs and yeast mixture. Work with the dough hook, beating slowly until the ingredients are mixed and then work at top speed for about 5 minutes. If you are kneading by hand, do so for 8–10 minutes. Add more flour if necessary so the dough is soft but not sticky. When sufficiently kneaded the dough will have the colour and texture of chamois leather.

Shape the dough into a ball, put it in an oiled bowl and turn it so the top is oiled. Cover it with a wet cloth and leave in a warm place for 1½–2 hours to rise until it has doubled in bulk. Work the dough lightly with your hands to knock out the air and then knead in the pieces of butter. Continue working in the mixer until all the butter is incorporated and the dough is smooth. Shape the dough into a ball again, oil it and cover it with a wet cloth. Keep it in the refrigerator for 6 hours or overnight: chilling makes it much easier to shape.

Butter two 1 kg (2 lb) loaf tins. Divide the dough in half and roll each piece to an 18 × 30 cm (7 × 12 inch) rectangle. Peel the sausages and set one lengthways on each piece of dough. Wrap the dough around the sausages and pinch the edges to seal them. Set the rolls, seam-side down, in the tins. Brush the tops with beaten egg glaze; be careful not to let any glaze run down the sides or the loaves will stick to the tins. Cover with a damp cloth and leave the brioches to rise in a warm place until the tins are full, about an hour. Preheat the oven.

Brush the loaves again with glaze and score them with a lattice with the point of a knife, or snip 'hedgehog points' with scissors. Bake in the oven for 40–45 minutes until the brioches are well browned and start to shrink from the sides of the tins. Turn the loaves out on a rack to cool. For serving, cut them in thick slices, discarding the ends. Sausage in brioche is best eaten on the day you make it, but it can be kept in the refrigerator for a day or two.

TERRINE DE LAPIN DE MADAME MILBERT

Madame Milbert's rabbit terrine   Serves 10–12

Preparation time: 35 minutes + 1 hour marinating + 2 hours cooking

1.5 kg (3 lb) rabbit, jointed

350 g (12 oz) streaky bacon, sliced

125 g (4 oz) cooked ham, diced

125 g (4 oz) pork fat, diced

3 tablespoons brandy

3 tablespoons Madeira or sherry

½ teaspoon ground allspice

a pinch of ground cloves

a pinch of ground nutmeg

500 g (1 lb) belly pork, minced

1 tablespoon salt, or to taste

2 teaspoons ground black pepper, or to taste

Oven temperature:
Gas Mark 4/180°C/350°F

Fifty yards from my kitchen, Madame Milbert's rabbits are munching away in the barn. Bred by the dozen in brown or white, dark or blue-eyed, flop-eared or perky, they must reconfirm Mendel's laws of heredity several times a year. On our family table they need to be disguised, hence the popularity of this terrine.

With a sharp-pointed knife, cut the meat from the legs of the rabbit, discarding the sinews. Cut the saddle meat from the backbone, keeping it in two pieces and then remove the fillets from under the ribs.

Finely chop one slice of bacon and fry it until the fat runs. Slice the saddle meat and fillets in thick strips, and cook them gently with the bacon until the meat is firm and white, 2–3 minutes. This prevents it shrinking and making hollows in the terrine.

Put the saddle and fillet meat in a bowl (do not use an aluminium one, which might mar the flavour) with the diced ham and pork fat, keeping the fried bacon aside. Add the brandy, Madeira or sherry, allspice, cloves and nutmeg, mix well, cover and leave to marinate for about an hour. Work the remaining rabbit meat through the fine blade of a mincer with the fried bacon. Drain the marinated meat, reserving the liquid. Stir the minced pork, diced ham and pork fat into the minced rabbit and then beat in salt, pepper and any marinade. Fry a small piece of the mixture and taste it: it should be highly seasoned.

Preheat the oven. Line the terrine mould with bacon, reserving 2–3 slices for the top. Spread a third of the minced mixture in a 1.75-litre (3-pint) terrine mould, arrange half of the strips of rabbit meat down the centre and cover with another layer of mixture. Add the rest of the rabbit meat and top with the remaining mixture. Cut the reserved bacon slices in strips and arrange in a lattice on top of the meat.

Fill a shallow pan such as a roasting tin to within 2.5 cm (1-inch) of the top with hot water. Set the mould in the water and bring it to the boil on top of the stove. Cook the terrine, uncovered, in the oven for 1½ – 2 hours or until firm; a skewer inserted in the centre should be hot to the touch when withdrawn and the juices should run clear. Let it cool to tepid and then press it overnight with a 1 kg (2 lb) weight on top. Keep the terrine in the refrigerator for at least two days and up to a week to allow the flavour to mellow. Unmould the terrine for serving, or serve it in the mould, cutting it in thick slices. Gherkin pickles are a mandatory accompaniment, with black olives too, if you like them.

Terrine de Gibier (Game terrine): When in doubt about the age and toughness of a piece of game, a terrine is one of the recipes I turn to. Strong flavours like hare or wood pigeon are particularly good. Follow the recipe for Terrine de Lapin de Madame Milbert, allowing about 500 g (1 lb) of trimmed meat to replace the rabbit.

OIE EN GELÉE DE MEURSAULT

Goose in white wine aspic   Serves 8–10 as a first course

Preparation time: 1 hour 15 minutes + 2½ hours cooking
+ 6 hours chilling

4 kg (8–9 lb) goose, with the giblets
1 pig's trotter, split
a bottle of full-bodied white burgundy
2 onions, quartered
2 carrots, quartered
a large bouquet garni
1 tablespoon black peppercorns
600 ml (1 pint) water, or more if needed
3–4 tablespoons marc or brandy
salt and pepper

Oven temperature:
Gas Mark 3/170°C/325°F

Since childhood, goose has been my favourite bird, so when I came across this recipe in an old cookbook from Dijon, I hastened to try it. The results, which resemble the coarse-textured pâté called 'rillettes', more than justify the use of a whole bottle of luxury wine such as Meursault, though any full-bodied Chardonnay will do. Two Emperor or Barbary ducks can be substituted for the goose.

Preheat the oven. Cut the goose in eight pieces (page 46), discarding the excess fat and skin. Put the pieces with the giblets in a heavy casserole, reserving the liver for another use as it will make the aspic bitter. Add the pig's trotter, wine, onions, carrots, bouquet garni, peppercorns, a little salt and enough water to cover. Fill a large shallow pan such as a roasting tin with hot water to within 2.5 cm (1 inch) of the top. Cover the casserole, set it in the water bath and bring it to the boil on top of the stove. Then cook it in the

Oie en Gelée de Meursault

24

Jambon Persillé du Morvan

oven until the meat falls from the bones, 2–2½ hours, adding more water if needed to keep the meat covered.

Remove the pieces of meat, strain the liquid and skim as much fat as possible from the surface. Add half the marc or brandy to the broth and boil it, skimming often, until it has reduced to 1 litre (1¾ pints). Add the remaining marc or brandy and taste: the liquid should be highly seasoned, particularly with pepper.

Remove the meat from the bones of both goose and pig's trotter, breaking up the larger pieces with two forks. Coarsely chop the skin and mix it with the meat. Put the meat mixture in a 1.5-litre (2½-pint) terrine mould or similar capacity glass bowl, and pour over the broth. Chill for at least 6 hours until set. Goose in aspic can be kept for up to a week in the refrigerator, but once cut it should be eaten within 2–3 days.

For serving, unmould the aspic, or leave it in the mould as you prefer. It is particularly good with Pain aux Noix (Walnut bread, page 84) and gherkin pickles.

Terrine de Lapin de Madame Milbert

JAMBON PERSILLÉ DU MORVAN

Parsleyed ham in aspic   Serves 10–12

Preparation time: soaking overnight + 40 minutes + 6 hours cooking + chilling

1.75 kg (4 lb) piece of raw gammon

1.75 kg (4 lb) bacon hock

2 pig's trotters, split

500 g (1 lb) veal bones

2 onions

1 leek, trimmed and split

3 sticks of celery

2 carrots

a bouquet garni

2 teaspoons black peppercorns

a bottle of dry white burgundy

2.5 litres (4½ pints) water, or more if needed

6 shallots, chopped finely

4–5 tablespoons chopped parsley

salt and pepper

The hilly Morvan district, lying roughly between Vézelay and Autun and now a National Park, is famous for its ham and dried sausages. In this recipe the ham is set in an aspic of white wine and parsley, forming a brilliant mosaic of pink and green. When this recipe is made there should be plenty of meat, as well as bones and skin to provide gelatine, so I like to use a piece of raw gammon as well as a bacon hock. Our local charcutier adds lots of finely chopped shallot to his parsleyed ham and that's what I have done here, though at home I sometimes opt for only parsley. So the colours can be fully appreciated, parsleyed ham is always moulded and served in a plain glass bowl.

If the gammon and bacon hock are very salty, soak them overnight in cold water, changing the water once or twice if possible. Blanch the gammon, hock, pig's trotters and veal bones by putting them in a large pot of cold water, bringing it to the boil and simmering for 5 minutes. Drain and rinse them with cold water. In a large, heavy pan put the gammon, hock, pig's trotters, veal bones, onions, leek, celery, carrots, bouquet garni, peppercorns, three-quarters of the wine and enough water to cover.

Bring everything slowly to the boil, skim well and simmer slowly, uncovered, for 5–6 hours or until the meat is tender enough to be pulled apart with a fork. Skim the broth often to keep the mixture clear, removing any fat from the surface. Add more water as necessary to keep the meat covered.

Let the mixture cool slightly and then lift out all the meat with a draining spoon. Discard the pig's trotters and the skin from the gammon and hock. Remove the meat from the bones, and set it aside. Skim any fat from the surface of the cooking liquid and boil it until it is reduced to

1.25 litres (2½ pints). Pull the meat into large chunks with two forks and mix it with the shallots. Strain the cooking broth through muslin and season it to taste. Scald the remaining wine by bringing it just to the boil and pour it over the parsley to give it a bright green colour; then mix the wine and parsley with the meat and shallots.

Put the meat in a 3-litre (5½-pint) glass bowl, spreading it level. Spoon over the aspic so it runs down between the pieces; it should barely cover the meat. Cover the bowl and chill the aspic until completely set, at least 6 hours.

Parsleyed ham can be kept for up to a week in the refrigerator but once cut it should be eaten within three days. It is served in the bowl, cut in slices like a terrine or in wedges like a cake. Gherkin pickles are a favourite accompaniment, with plenty of crusty bread.

EGGS AND CHEESE

Since I've lived in Burgundy, I've become spoiled by a constant supply of fresh eggs from the farmyard. They inspire simple little supper dishes like eggs baked *en cocotte* with sweet baby onions. When Chef Chambrette comes down from Paris, the classic dish of poached eggs in *meurette* red wine sauce, now enjoying a renaissance, appears as a first course.

The variety of local cheeses made within a hundred-kilometer radius of home is an even greater temptation. From the north come creamy Brie and Coulommiers, while the greatest of all is Epoisses, sold at every stage of ripeness to a mellow, redolent cream. Add to these a dozen anonymous types of goat's cheese and it's easy to understand why Burgundians tend to eat their cheese rather than cook with it. Gougères (page 31), however, are the exception.

CLAQUERET

Fresh cheese with herbs	Serves 6–8

Preparation time: 15 minutes

350 g (12 oz) soft cream cheese

5–6 tablespoons crème fraîche (page 7) or double cream

2 tablespoons white wine

1 tablespoon vegetable oil

2 cloves of garlic, chopped finely

2 tablespoons chopped parsley

2 tablespoons chopped chives

salt and pepper

In southern Burgundy and the Lyonnais, even modest restaurants offer the choice of either a tray of aged cheeses or of fresh cheese which comes with sugar or chopped garlic and herbs for flavouring. This version keeps well and is good served with boiled potatoes, toast or french bread.

If the cheese is very stiff, work it through a sieve. Beat in enough *crème fraîche* or cream to make a soft spread and then beat in the wine, oil, garlic, parsley and chives with salt and pepper to taste. The cheese can be kept for up to a week in the refrigerator but serve claqueret at room temperature.

Claqueret with a selection of Burgundian cheeses

OEUFS EN MEURETTE

Poached eggs in red wine sauce | Serves 4 as a main course

Preparation and cooking time: 45 minutes

a bottle of red burgundy

475 ml (16 fl oz) veal stock

8 fresh eggs

For the sauce:

15 g (½ oz) unsalted butter

1 onion, sliced thinly

1 carrot, sliced thinly

1 stick of celery, sliced thinly

1 clove of garlic, crushed

a bouquet garni

6 black peppercorns

beurre manié made with
20 g (¾ oz) unsalted butter
and 15 g (½ oz) flour
(page 8)

For the garnish:

25 g (1 oz) unsalted butter

75 g (3 oz) mushrooms,
quartered

16–20 baby onions, peeled

75 g (3 oz) streaky bacon,
cut in lardons (thin strips)
and blanched if salty
(see Note, below)

8 round fried bread croûtes,
6 cm (2½ inches) in
diameter (page 7)

salt and pepper

'Meurette' is a red wine sauce and one of the grand Burgundian traditions, combining bacon and onions with whatever happens to be the local vintage. Red wine contributes a fruity richness that is totally lacking in a white wine sauce.

To poach the eggs, bring the wine and stock to a boil in a sauté pan or shallow saucepan. Break four eggs, one by one, into places where the liquid bubbles. Lower the heat and poach the eggs for 3–4 minutes until the yolk is fairly firm but still soft to the touch. Transfer the eggs to paper towels to drain and poach the rest. Strain the cooking liquid and set it aside.

For the sauce, melt the butter, add the onion, carrot and celery and cook them gently until they are soft but not brown. Add the poaching liquid, garlic, bouquet garni and peppercorns and simmer for 20–25 minutes until the liquid is reduced by half.

Meanwhile, cook the garnish. Melt half the butter in a frying pan and sauté the mushrooms until tender. Remove them, add the remaining butter and sauté the onions for 10–15 minutes until they are tender and lightly browned, shaking the pan so they colour evenly. Add them to the mushrooms. Finally fry the bacon until it has browned and add it to the mushrooms and onions, discarding the fat from the pan.

To thicken the sauce, first reheat it if necessary and then whisk in the kneaded butter, a piece at a time, until the sauce is thick enough to coat a spoon lightly. Strain it over the garnish and season to taste with salt and pepper. If you are preparing ahead, put the eggs in a bowl of cold water. The eggs, sauce and garnish can be kept for up to two days in the refrigerator.

To finish, reheat the sauce and garnish on top of the stove if necessary. Reheat the eggs by putting them in hot water for 1 minute and then draining them on paper towels. Set the eggs on the croûtes and put them on a serving dish or on individual plates, allowing two each. Coat the eggs completely with the sauce.

Note: To cut bacon in lardons is a typical technique of French cooking. French bacon is streaky and quite fat and is seldom found sliced. It may be salted, or both salted and smoked, and generally needs blanching to remove the salt. For lardons, cut the bacon in 5 mm (¼-inch) slices and then cut the slices across into short strips. To blanch lardons, put them in a pan of cold water, bring to the boil and simmer for 2–3 minutes. Drain, rinse with cold water and drain thoroughly again.

GOUGÈRES

| Cheese choux puffs | Makes fifteen 10 cm (4-inch) gougères |

Preparation time: 25 minutes + 30 minutes cooking

175 ml (6 fl oz) water

½ teaspoon salt

75 g (3 oz) unsalted butter, plus extra for greasing

3½ oz (100 g) plain flour

3–4 eggs

60 g (2½ oz) Gruyère cheese, diced

ground black pepper

To finish:

1 egg, lightly beaten with ½ teaspoon salt

2 tablespoons grated Gruyère cheese

Oven temperature:
Gas Mark 7/220°C/425°F

At least three towns – Sens, Tonnerre and Avallon – claim credit for these cheese puffs, but you'll find them all over Burgundy whenever a glass of wine is served. Large or small, a gougère should be crisp on the outside, soft within, and served warm. The name is a corruption of Gruyère, which should be used to make them.

Preheat the oven and butter two baking sheets.

To make the dough, heat the water, salt and butter in a saucepan until the butter is melted. Bring it just to the boil and take the pan from the heat. At once add all the flour and beat vigorously with a wooden spatula until the mixture is smooth and comes away from the sides of the pan in a ball, about 1 minute. Return the pan to the heat and cook the dough for ½–1 minute, stirring constantly. Take it from the heat and let it cool slightly.

Beat one egg until it is mixed and set it aside. Beat the remaining eggs into the warm dough one at a time, beating the dough thoroughly after adding each one. Beat in the last egg little

31

by little, adding enough to make a shiny mixture which just falls from the spoon. This consistency is important: too little egg makes the dough heavy, but with too much it will not be firm enough to shape. Stir in the diced cheese with pepper to taste.

Using two spoons, shape the dough into 5 cm (2-inch) mounds on the baking sheets, setting them well apart so the dough has room to rise. Brush the gougères with egg glaze and sprinkle them with grated cheese. Bake them in the oven for 25–30 minutes until they are golden brown and crisp on the outside.

Gougères can be baked up to 8 hours ahead and warmed in the oven just before serving.

OEUFS EN COCOTTE LYONNAISE

Eggs in ramekins with croûtons and onions   Serves 8 as a first course

Preparation time: 20 minutes + 15 minutes cooking

50 g (2 oz) unsalted butter

175 g (6 oz) baby white onions or spring onions, sliced

6 slices of white bread, fried as croûtons (page 7)

8 eggs

125 ml (4 fl oz) double cream

salt and pepper

Oven temperature:
Gas Mark 5/190°C/375°F

Unless you are preparing the garnish in advance, preheat the oven. Melt the butter in a frying pan and fry the onions until they are golden. Season them with salt and pepper and spread them in the bottom of eight ramekins. Spread the croûtons on top of the onions and sprinkle them with a little salt and pepper. This can be prepared in advance.

Fill a large shallow pan such as a roasting tin with hot water to within 2.5 cm (1 inch) of the top. Break an egg into each ramekin and spoon over the cream. Set them in the water bath and bring it to the boil on top of the stove. Cook the eggs in the oven for 10–11 minutes depending on the thickness of the dishes, until the whites are almost set; the eggs will continue cooking in the hot dishes when you take them from the oven. When served, the whites should just be set and the yolks soft.

Gougères
Oeufs en Meurette
Oeufs en Cocotte Lyonnaise

Oeufs au Plat Lyonnaise: If we have a good many guests, instead of baking eggs *en cocotte*, I spread the onions and croûtons in a gratin dish, break the eggs on top, add the cream and bake them *au plat* in the oven without a water bath. It takes nearly 15 minutes for the whites to set, leaving the yolks soft.

OMELETTE BOURGUIGNONNE

Snail omelette with walnuts   Serves 2

Preparation and cooking time: 20 minutes

125 g (4 oz) canned snails
45 g (1½ oz) unsalted butter
1–2 cloves of garlic, chopped
25 g (1 oz) walnuts, chopped coarsely
2 tablespoons chopped parsley
5–6 eggs
salt and pepper

This recipe is very versatile: I've made the omelette without the snails and I've served snails on their own with a walnut, garlic and parsley butter and no omelette. Both were as delicious as the original.

Drain and rinse the snails and cut them in 2–3 pieces. Melt half the butter in a frying pan, add the snails, garlic, salt and pepper and cook them gently for 4–5 minutes. Take the pan from the heat and stir in the walnuts and parsley. The snails can be kept chilled for up to a day.

To cook the omelette: whisk the eggs with a little salt and pepper until they are well mixed. Warm the snail mixture over a low heat. Heat the remaining butter in a 22–25 cm (9–10-inch) omelette pan until it stops spluttering. Add the eggs and stir briskly with a fork, pulling the cooked egg from the sides to the centre of the pan. After 10 seconds, stir in the snail mixture and continue cooking for 5–10 seconds longer until the mixture is almost as thick as scrambled eggs. Leave the omelette on the heat until browned on the bottom and still soft on top if you like a runny omelette, or almost firm if you like it well done.

Fold the omelette, tipping the pan away from you and turning the edge with a fork. Half roll, half slide the omelette on to a warm serving dish so it lands folded in three. Serve at once.

FISH

Lying as Burgundy does at the heart of France, it is hardly surprising that good fish is lacking. Yet only a generation or two ago great rivers like the Rhône, the Saône and the Loire produced an abundance of freshwater fish. The humbler varieties like perch, carp and tench were reserved for stew, while a whole range of traditional dishes call for salmon, trout, pike, frogs' legs and the succulent little red–clawed crayfish from the Dombes region near Bresse, which is studded with lakes.

Nowadays, fish farms are trying to fill the gaps in supply. I've noticed, however, that more and more restaurants are turning to sea fish and that is what I would suggest in many of the following recipes. Bream is a good substitute for carp, for instance, lemon sole or plaice can replace perch and hake or whiting can be used instead of pike. Bream and pike can be ordered from Sainsbury fresh fish counters. Ask at the fish counter for advice.

Note: All the serving quantities in the recipes in this chapter are as main course dishes.

TRUITE SAUMONÉE EN GELÉE AU CHIROUBLES

Salmon trout in red wine aspic   Serves 10

Preparation and cooking time: 2 hours

a whole salmon trout, about 3 kg (6–8 lb) in weight

fish stock made with 500 g (1 lb) fish bones and heads, a bottle of red burgundy, 2 sliced onions, 12 black peppercorns, a bouquet garni and 1.5 litres (2¼ pints) water (page 8)

25 g (1 oz) or 3 envelopes gelatine

Why aspic is not made more often with red instead of white wine, I cannot imagine; it emerges a rich crimson, a perfect foil for this festive whole trout. The recipe may seem long, but it is ideal for a party as it can be completed a day in advance. A light Beaujolais-type wine is best for making the aspic. Here I've suggested a garnish of tomato baskets filled with cucumber, but stuffed eggs or simple salads of cucumber and potato vinaigrette would be equally suitable.

Wash the fish and set it, stomach down, along the side of a large round or oval casserole so the

35

10 medium-size tomatoes	
1 large cucumber	
3 tablespoons wine vinegar	
salt and pepper	

To garnish:

a bunch of watercress

back is curved. Strain over the fish stock; the fish should be completely covered, but if it is not add more water.

Cover the casserole and bring the liquid slowly to a simmer taking about 20 minutes. Poach the fish for 15–20 minutes (allow 5 minutes total cooking time, including bringing to the boil, per pound of fish). If the liquid is allowed to boil, the aspic will be cloudy. Leave the trout to cool in the liquid until tepid and then drain it, reserving the liquid. Peel the skin from the fish while it is still warm, so it does not stick. Remove the fins and scoop out the small bones along the back-bone, leaving the head and tail. Refrigerate the fish, setting it on a rack with a pan underneath.

Strain the poaching liquid through a double layer of muslin rinsed in hot water. Pour about a cup of the liquid into a small bowl and let it cool to tepid. Sprinkle over the gelatine and leave for about 5 minutes until the gelatine is spongy. Boil the remaining liquid until it has reduced to 1.25 litres (2¼ pints). Add the softened gelatine to the hot liquid, stirring until it has melted. Leave the aspic to cool and then season it to taste.

For the garnish: halve the tomatoes and scoop out the seeds with a teaspoon. Sprinkle the insides with salt and pepper, and leave them upside down to drain. Peel, de-seed and dice the cucumbers, sprinkle them with salt and leave them for 30 minutes in a colander to draw out their juices. Rinse them with cold water, drain thoroughly and mix with the vinegar. Fill the tomatoes with the cucumber and chill them.

To coat the fish with aspic, set a cup or two of the aspic in a bowl over ice and stir gently until the aspic is almost oily in consistency and ice cold. It will set quickly at this point, so work fast. Take the fish from the refrigerator and spoon the aspic over it, splashing so it spreads out well. Chill the fish again; then cool more aspic and add another coating. (If the aspic in the bowl sets, melt it over a low heat, and cool again over ice.)

Truite Saumonée en Gelée au Chiroubles

Spoon a shallow layer of melted aspic into a serving dish (if possible use a silver or stainless steel dish, so the colour is reflected) and chill it until set. Coat the filled tomatoes with chilled aspic also. Chill any remaining aspic in the bowl and then turn it on to a sheet of wet greaseproof paper and chop it coarsely with a wet knife. The whole coating process can be speeded up by chilling in the freezer, but if it gets too cold, the aspic will crystallise and destroy all your hard work.

To assemble the dish: transfer the trout on to the serving dish lined with aspic. Pile chopped aspic at the base of the fish and arrange the tomatoes around the edge. The dish can be kept, loosely covered with plastic wrap, in the refrigerator for up to 24 hours. Just before serving, add the watercress. Serve a plain or herb mayonnaise separately.

CARPE EN MEURETTE

Baked carp in red wine   Serves 4

Preparation time: 35 minutes + 4 hours marinating + 25 minutes cooking

a whole carp weighing about 1.2 kg (2½–3 lb), cleaned, with the head
2 cloves of garlic, chopped finely
1 shallot, chopped finely
a bottle of red burgundy
a bouquet garni
For the garnish:
25 g (1 oz) unsalted butter, plus extra for greasing
150 g (5 oz) streaky bacon, cut in lardons (thin strips) and blanched if salty (page 31)
15–20 baby onions
1 tablespoon water

Carp had always been a disappointment until I tasted it 'en meurette', for this powerful red wine sauce with bacon and onions perfectly suits its robust, somewhat coarse texture. Indeed, so highly prized is a fine carp in Burgundy that in the nineteenth century when the fishermen of Nevers presented their catch to the departmental governor they were given a free ticket to the city ball. This could also be made with bream.

Scale the fish and remove the fins. Trim the tail to a 'V' and wash it thoroughly. Slash the fish 2–3 times on both sides so it cooks evenly. Spread the garlic and shallot in a baking dish, lay the fish on top and pour over the wine. Add the bouquet garni and sprinkle with salt and pepper. Cover the fish and leave it in the refrigerator to marinate for up to 4 hours.

For the garnish: melt half the butter and fry the bacon until it is lightly browned and then

beurre manié made with 40 g
(1½ oz) unsalted butter and
25 g (1 oz) flour (page 8)

2 tablespoons brandy

25 g (1 oz) cold butter, cut
in pieces

8 triangular or heart-shaped
fried bread croûtes (page 7)

2 tablespoons chopped
parsley

salt and pepper

Oven temperature:
Gas Mark 4/180°C/350°F

drain it. Put the onions in a pan with the
remaining butter and a tablespoon of water. Add
seasoning, cover and cook gently for 10–15
minutes until the onions are tender. Shake the
pan occasionally and do not let them brown.
Add them to the bacon. The garnish can be
prepared at the same time as the fish.

To cook the fish: preheat the oven. Cover the
fish with buttered foil and bake it in the
marinade until it just flakes easily, 20–25
minutes. Transfer it to a serving dish and keep it
warm. Strain the cooking liquid into a saucepan
and boil until it has reduced to 475 ml (16 fl oz).
Whisk in the *beurre manié*, a piece at a time, until
the sauce lightly coats a spoon. Stir in the brandy,
add the onions and bacon and taste for seasoning.
Keep the sauce warm for 5 minutes so the
flavours mellow and then stir in the butter in
pieces.

Dip points of the croûtes in the sauce and then
in chopped parsley and arrange them around the
dish. Spoon the sauce and garnish over the fish
to coat it, sprinkle the fish with the remaining
chopped parsley and serve. I find this dish
delicious with sorrel purée, but that's a personal
taste.

POCHOUSE

Fish stew with white wine and cream   Serves 6–8

Preparation and cooking time: 1½ hours

2 kg (4½ lb) mixed whole
freshwater fish, including
eel, scaled and cleaned

2 tablespoons marc or cognac

300 ml (½ pint) white
burgundy

a bouquet garni

125 g (4 oz) streaky bacon,
cut in lardons (thin strips)
and blanched if salty
(page 31)

*Pochouse is a Burgundian staple. (The name comes
from 'pauche', the fisherman's sack for his catch.)
There are many versions: Pochouse may be a thin
broth or a rich stew, more sauce than soup; the fish
may be left whole or taken from the bone. No matter
how it is made, it should contain the widest possible
range of fish, with some eel for richness. White wine is
the characteristic of Pochouse, preferably a local
Chablis or Aligoté. When made with red wine, the
dish becomes 'poisson en meurette' and resembles Carpe
en Meurette (Baked carp in red wine, page 38).*

Onions and bacon are the usual flavourings for

1 onion, sliced thinly
1 bulb of fennel, sliced thinly
2 cloves of garlic, chopped finely
fish stock made with heads from the fish, 1 onion, sliced thinly, a bouquet garni, 1 teaspoon black peppercorns, 125 ml (4 fl oz) white wine and 1.25 litres (2¼ pints) water (page 8)
beurre manié made with 40 g (1½ oz) unsalted butter and 25 g (1 oz) flour (page 8)
125 ml (4 fl oz) crème fraîche (page 7) or double cream
a few drops of lemon juice
salt and pepper
To garnish:
2 tablespoons chopped parsley
10–12 heart-shaped fried bread croûtes (page 7)

Pochouse but some cooks add a bit of sorrel and the great Fernand Point, father of the new-style cooking movement, living in Vienne with easy access to the Mediterranean, included fennel and tomatoes in an echo of bouillabaisse. In this recipe I follow Point's example, adding fennel to balance the richness of what can be an overwhelming sauce. My favourite accompaniment is boiled new potatoes, though they are by no means traditional.

Cut the eel into 5 cm (2-inch) slices and remove the skin; cut the other fish in 2 cm (¾-inch) slices. Wash the fish, pat them dry with paper towels and put the pieces in a bowl with the marc or cognac, wine, bouquet garni, salt and pepper.

Fry the bacon in a tablespoon of the butter until it is lightly browned and then drain it. Melt the remaining butter in a pan, add the onion, the fennel and the garlic, press a piece of foil on top and cook gently until the vegetables are very soft, 15–20 minutes. Do not let the vegetables brown. Add the fish stock and bring it to the boil.

Meanwhile, in a large pan arrange the fish in layers, eel at the bottom followed by the firmer fish and ending with delicate fish such as trout. Pour over the marinade with the bouquet garni and the fish stock with vegetables and simmer until the fish flakes easily, about 10 minutes. Lift out the pieces of fish, reserving the broth, and discard the bouquet garni. Purists like to leave the fish with skin on the bone, and so, I must confess, do idle cooks like me. On more formal occasions, however, guests much appreciate having the work done for them. Whether or not you have removed the bones, keep the fish warm.

To finish: bring the broth to a boil and whisk in *beurre manié*, a piece at a time, until the broth is the consistency of thin cream. Stir in the cream and bacon and taste for seasoning, adding a few drops of lemon juice. Arrange the pieces of fish in a tureen or individual bowls, pour over the sauce and sprinkle with parsley. Serve the croûtes separately, or perch them at the side of the bowl.

QUENELLES AUX CREVETTES

Fish dumplings with prawn sauce   Serves 8

Preparation time: 1 hour + 15 minutes cooking

1 kg (2 lb) pike, whiting, trout or other firm fish, including the heads

2 egg whites, beaten until frothy

300 ml (½ pint) crème fraîche (page 7) or double cream

For the prawn sauce:

60 g (2½ oz) unsalted butter, plus extra for greasing

½ onion, chopped finely

½ carrot, chopped finely

750 g (1½ lb) large raw prawns in their shells

3 tablespoons brandy

4 tablespoons white wine

a bouquet garni

fish stock made with fish bones, 1 onion, sliced thinly, a bouquet garni, 1 teaspoon black peppercorns, 125 ml (4 fl oz) white wine and 1 litre (1¾ pints) water (page 8)

30 g (1¼ oz) flour

300 ml (½ pint) crème fraîche (page 7) or double cream

½ teaspoon tomato purée

a pinch of cayenne pepper

salt and pepper

Oven temperature:
Gas Mark 5/190°C/375°F

'Quenelles' fish dumplings are one of the delicacies of Lyon, at their finest served with a 'Nantua' sauce of crayfish from the foothills of the Alps. This recipe made with prawns is a close copy, flavoured with the requisite touches of brandy and cayenne. The quenelles are my own variation, as I find this mousseline mixture of fish, egg white and cream is both lighter and easier to make than the traditional flour-thickened dumpling. The fish must be fresh (frozen fish is too wet) and it is puréed in the food processor to avoid hard work by hand.

Fillet and skin the fish, reserving the heads and bones for the stock, or ask at the fish counter for this to be done for you. There should be 500 g (1 lb) fillets.

Wash the fillets, pat them dry and purée them in a food processor or work them twice through the fine blade of a mincer. Put the fish in a bowl and set it in a pan of iced water. With a wooden spoon, beat in the egg whites a little at a time. Season the mixture with salt and pepper and then beat in the *crème fraîche* or cream in three or four portions. The mixture should be quite stiff, but if it seems soft, chill it again very thoroughly. Taste it for seasoning.

To poach the quenelles: bring a large shallow pan of salted water almost to a boil. Using two dessert spoons dipped in the water, shape an oval of quenelle mixture and drop it into the water. If it starts to break up, add more lightly beaten egg white to the mixture and beat for another few minutes over ice. Shape the remaining mixture into ovals and drop them into the water. Poach them just below boiling point until firm, 6–8 minutes depending on size. Lift them out and drain on paper towels.

For the prawn sauce: melt 25 g (1 oz) of the butter in a shallow pan and fry the onion and carrot until soft but not brown. Add the prawns and sauté over a high heat for 1 minute. Add 2 tablespoons of the brandy and flame it. Add the white wine, bouquet garni, fish stock, salt and pepper and simmer until the prawns are cooked, 2–4 minutes depending on size. Remove the prawns and shell them. Return the shells to the pan and continue simmering for 10 minutes. Strain the liquid, pressing hard to extract all the juice from the shells.

Melt the remaining butter in a saucepan, whisk in the flour and cook until it is foaming. Whisk in the prawn stock and bring the sauce to the boil, whisking constantly until it thickens. Simmer for 5 minutes or until it lightly coats a spoon. Whisk in the cream and tomato purée and bring the sauce just back to the boil. Take it from the heat, whisk in the cayenne and remaining brandy and season to taste.

Butter eight individual gratin dishes, arrange three or four quenelles in each one and scatter the prawns on top. Coat the quenelles and prawns generously with sauce. If tightly covered they can be kept for up to two days in the refrigerator.

To finish, preheat the oven and bake the quenelles for 10–15 minutes or until browned and slightly puffed up. Serve them very hot in the gratin dishes.

TRUITES MONTBARDOISE

Trout stuffed with spinach and shallots   Serves 6

Preparation time: 20 minutes + 15 minutes + 40 minutes cooking

750 g (1½ lb) fresh or frozen and thawed leaf spinach

175 g (6 oz) unsalted butter, plus extra for greasing

8 shallots, chopped finely

2 cloves of garlic, chopped

6 tablespoons crème fraîche (page 7) or double cream

When you are cleaning the trout, make as small a slit in the stomach as possible, so a handy pocket is left for the stuffing.

To make the stuffing, tear the stems from the fresh spinach, wash the leaves thoroughly in several changes of cold water and drain them. Pack the spinach in a saucepan, add 1.5 cm (½ inch) of water and cover. Cook over a medium heat, stirring occasionally, for about

zest of 1 lemon, grated

6 tablespoons chopped parsley

6 tablespoons fresh breadcrumbs

grated nutmeg

6 whole trout

10–12 sprigs of fresh thyme

1 bottle Aligoté or dry white burgundy

salt and pepper

Oven temperature:
Gas Mark 4/180°C/350°F

5 minutes or until the spinach is wilted and just tender. Drain it in a colander, rinse it with cold water and drain again. Press the spinach in your fists to extract all the water. Chop it finely by hand or in a food processor. Prepare frozen spinach as directed on the packet. Melt 25 g (1 oz) of the butter in the saucepan, add half the shallots and the garlic and cook for 30 seconds. Stir in the spinach and cook it for 2–3 minutes until dry. Add the *crème fraîche* or cream with the lemon zest, parsley, breadcrumbs, nutmeg and salt and pepper to taste. Chill the stuffing for 15 minutes.

Meanwhile, clean and scale the trout pulling out and discarding the gills and then fill the cavities of the trout with the stuffing through the gills using a teaspoon.

Butter a flameproof dish and sprinkle it with the remaining shallots. Slash the trout 2–3 times on each side so they cook evenly and lay them in a baking dish. Insert sprigs of thyme in the slashes, pour over the wine and cover the trout with foil. They can be prepared to this stage up to 4 hours ahead and refrigerated, if you chill the stuffing before putting it in the fish.

To cook the trout, first preheat the oven. Bring the trout with the wine just to the boil on top of the stove and put them in the oven. Bake for 15–20 minutes or until the trout just flake easily. Transfer them to a serving dish or individual plates, cover them and keep them warm because the sauce takes about 20 minutes to reduce.

To make the sauce: strain the cooking liquid into a saucepan and boil until it has reduced to 4 tablespoons. Take it from the heat and whisk in the remaining butter in small pieces, taking the pan on and off the heat so the butter softens and thickens the sauce creamily without melting to oil. Taste the sauce for seasoning and spoon it over the fish. Serve at once.

SUPRÊME DE BROCHET MÈRE BRAZIER

Pike fillets with bacon, mushroom and cream sauce   Serves 4

Preparation time: 25 minutes + 8 hours marinating + 20 minutes cooking

150 g (5 oz) streaky bacon, cut in lardons (thin strips) and blanched if salty (page 31)

50 g (2 oz) unsalted butter

1 kg (2 lb) fillets of pike

3 shallots, chopped finely

4 tablespoons brandy

4 tablespoons Madeira or sherry

250 ml (8 fl oz) dry white wine

a bouquet garni

250 g (8 oz) mushrooms, sliced thinly

175 ml (6 fl oz) crème fraîche (page 7) or double cream

salt and pepper

Oven temperature:
Gas Mark 4/180°C/350°F

Mère Brazier was one of the great women cooks of Lyon. 'With the death of Mère Brazier disappears a style of cooking that is simple, honest, rigorous, and without pretention' sighs Paul Bocuse, the 'emperor' and founder of nouvelle cuisine, who trained with her for three years as a commis assistant cook. Any well flavoured white fish such as hake or haddock can take the place of pike in this dish.

Cook the bacon strips in 1 tablespoon of the butter for 2–3 minutes until browned and then drain them. Cut small slashes in the fish and insert the bacon strips. Sprinkle the shallots in a shallow ovenproof baking dish (not an aluminium one which would mar the flavour), lay the fish on top and pour over the brandy, Madeira or sherry and wine. Sprinkle with pepper and add the bouquet garni. Cover and leave in the refrigerator to marinate for 8 to 12 hours.

Preheat the oven. Spread the mushrooms around the fish and bake it in the oven for 20–25 minutes until the fish flakes easily. Transfer the fish to a serving dish and keep it warm. Add the *crème fraîche* or cream to the baking dish and boil until the sauce is well reduced and concentrated. Take it from the heat, discard the bouquet garni and whisk in the remaining butter, a few pieces at a time. Taste the sauce for seasoning and spoon it over the fish. Serve at once.

Suprême de Brochet Mère Brazier

Truites Montbardoise

Quenelles aux
Crevettes

45

POULTRY AND GAME

The aristocrats among French chickens come from Bresse, just east of the Côte d'Or wine country. Here, in the bracing foothills of the Alps, birds are reared under a strict regime of maize and outdoor exercise with such success that a *poulet de Bresse*, recognisable by its blue feet, costs three times as much as an ordinary chicken.

I rarely make the investment, for I find that our local market lady offers excellent fresh birds, together with trimmings like chicken livers, boned breasts and rolled turkey roasts in the winter season. No matter what the recipe, I tend to buy a big bird, finding it richer and more economical than little young ones. Indeed, one of the rare local treats is a full-blown cock bird or a hen past its prime for laying eggs, plump-bosomed and extraordinarily tasty when cooked for hours in wine, as in the recipe for Poularde au Vin Nuitonne (Chicken in red wine sauce, page 58).

Jointing poultry into eight

A number of the following recipes call for a bird to be cut in eight pieces, which is easily done by the following method.

With a heavy knife, first cut off the wing tips. Cut between the leg and body of the bird, following the outline of the thigh, until the leg joint is visible. Locate the oyster meat lying against the backbone, and cut around it so it remains attached to the thigh. Twist the leg sharply outwards to break the thigh joint. Cut each leg from the body, including the oyster meat.

With a knife or poultry shears, cut away the backbone and cut along the breastbone to halve the carcass. The bird is now in four pieces. To cut it into eight, divide each breast in half, cutting diagonally through the meat and then through the breast and rib bones so a portion of breast meat is cut off with the wing. Trim the rib bones.

Cut the legs in half through the joint, using the white line of fat on the underside as a guide. When cooking, add the backbone and wingtips with the other pieces to help flavour the sauce.

MAGRET DE CANARD AUX BAIES DE CASSIS

Duck breast with blackcurrants   Serves 4

Preparation and cooking time: 45 minutes

4 duck breasts, or two small whole ducks

1 tablespoon vegetable oil

25 g (1 oz) unsalted butter

For the sauce:

125 g (4 oz) fresh black-currants, or canned or frozen and thawed blackcurrants

3 tablespoons cassis (blackcurrant liqueur)

3 shallots, chopped finely

250 ml (8 fl oz) red burgundy

125 ml (4 fl oz) red wine vinegar

250 ml (8 fl oz) veal or chicken stock

2 teaspoons arrowroot mixed to a paste with 2 tablespoons water

40 g (1½ oz) unsalted butter, cut in pieces

salt and pepper

To garnish:

a bunch of watercress

The nouvelle cuisine custom of serving duck breast (magret) on its own rather like a steak has proved so popular that boned breasts are now routinely available in French supermarkets. Magrets are easy to prepare at home from a whole duck but then the legs are left. Try using them in Ragoût de Cuisses de Canard aux Navets (Stew of duck legs with turnips, page 48).

To remove the breasts if you are using whole ducks, first lift the neck skin, and, with a sharp knife, cut out the wishbone. Remove the legs by cutting through the skin between the leg and breast, grasp the leg and, with a sharp twist, break the joint. Cut through it to sever it. Remove each breast by sliding the knife between meat and bone. Leave the skin on the two breasts or remove it, as you prefer.

Heat the oil and butter in a frying pan. Season the duck breasts with salt and pepper and fry them skin-side down over a brisk heat for about 5 minutes until they are thoroughly browned. Turn them and brown the other side, allowing 8 minutes total cooking for rare meat or longer if you prefer it well done. If the skin has been discarded, shorten the cooking time by about 2 minutes. Remove the breasts and keep them warm.

Pick over fresh blackcurrants or if you are using canned or frozen berries, drain them. Put the blackcurrants in a pan with the cassis liqueur and let them simmer for 1–2 minutes. Fresh blackcurrants will take 10 minutes or more to cook until tender and you may need to add a little water. The blackcurrants and uncooked duck breasts can be kept for up to 8 hours in the refrigerator.

To make the sauce, discard all but a half tablespoon of fat from the pan. Add the shallots and cook them until they are soft. Add the wine and vinegar and boil until they have reduced to about three tablespoons. Add the stock and bring it to the boil. Re-mix the arrowroot paste if it has separated and whisk in enough to make the boiling sauce lightly coat a spoon. Stir in the blackcurrants and taste for seasoning. Take the sauce from the heat and add the 40 g (1½ oz) butter, swirling the pan so it melts creamily. Keep the sauce warm.

Cut each magret in 4–5 thin diagonal slices and arrange them in a fan on individual plates. Spoon over the sauce and decorate each plate with watercress. Serve the duck with Crapiaux Morvandiaux (Grated potato pancakes, page 72) or Soufflé de Marrons (Chestnut soufflé, page 71).

RAGOÛT DE CUISSES DE CANARD AUX NAVETS

Stew of duck legs with turnips	Serves 4

Preparation time: 35 minutes + 1¾ hours cooking

1 tablespoon vegetable oil	*Some cooks grill duck legs to serve with the breast in recipes like Magret de Canard aux Baies de Cassis (Duck breast with blackcurrants, page 47), but I find them rather tough and prefer to cook them separately in a traditional ragoût like this one. It can be served at the same time as the breasts or on a separate occasion. Rabbit is good cooked this way too.*
4 duck legs or 1 whole duck, cut in 8 pieces (page 46)	
500 g (1 lb) onions, sliced	
15 g (½ oz) flour	
175 ml (6 fl oz) red burgundy	
250 ml (8 fl oz) veal or chicken stock	In a sauté pan or shallow casserole heat the oil and sauté the duck pieces or legs, skin-side down, for 10–15 minutes until the fat is rendered. This is important if the finished dish is not to be greasy. Remove the duck and pour off all but two tablespoons of fat. Add the onions and cook until they have browned. Stir in the flour and cook for 1 minute. Add the wine,
a bouquet garni	
2 shallots, chopped	
2 cloves of garlic, chopped	

Ragoût de Cuisses de Canard aux Navets
Magret de Canard aux Baies de Cassis

500 g (1 lb) small white turnips, cut in wedges
25 g (1 oz) unsalted butter
1 teaspoon caster sugar
1 tablespoon chopped parsley
salt and pepper

stock, bouquet garni, shallots, garlic, salt and pepper. Replace the duck, cover the pan or casserole and simmer until the duck is tender and the meat is almost falling from the bone, 1¼– 1½ hours.

For the garnish: put the turnips, butter and sugar in a pan, season with salt and pepper and add water to cover. Simmer uncovered until the turnips are tender and all the water is evaporated, 20–25 minutes. Continue cooking the turnips until they are glazed and browned, shaking the pan frequently so they colour evenly.

Add the glazed turnips to the duck and simmer, uncovered, for 10–15 minutes more. Discard the bouquet garni and taste the sauce for seasoning. The ragoût can be refrigerated for up to three days. Reheat it on top of the stove, transfer it to a serving dish and sprinkle with parsley for serving.

POULET SAUTÉ AU VINAIGRE DE VIN

Sauté of chicken with vinegar, tomato and garlic   Serves 4

Preparation and cooking time: 1 hour 20 minutes

1.5 kg (3 lb) roasting chicken, cut in 8 pieces (page 46)
60 g (2½ oz) unsalted butter
15 cloves of garlic, unpeeled
300 ml (½ pint) red wine vinegar
500 g (1 lb) ripe tomatoes, chopped coarsely
1 tablespoon tomato purée
a bouquet garni
250 ml (8 fl oz) chicken stock, or more if needed
salt and pepper

Chicken with vinegar is an ancient recipe, dating from the middle ages before lemon was available to add acidity. This version is deceptive: though it contains fifteen cloves of garlic, their flavour blends and becomes almost undetectable in the sauce. I like to make this in summer, when tomatoes are at their best and hot weather makes the slight sharpness of the sauce welcome.

Season the chicken pieces with salt and pepper. In a large sauté pan with a lid heat 25 g (1 oz) butter until it foams. Add the pieces of chicken, skin-side down, starting with the legs and thighs because they need the longest cooking. When they begin to brown, add the wing pieces and finally the breast. After about 10 minutes or when all are brown, turn them over and brown the other side for 1–2 minutes.

Add the garlic, cover the pan and cook over a

low heat for 10 minutes. Holding the cover on the pan to prevent the chicken falling out, pour off the excess fat. Add the vinegar to the pan and simmer, uncovered, for about 10–15 minutes until the sauce is well reduced. Add the tomatoes, tomato purée and bouquet garni, cover and simmer for 10 minutes more, or until the chicken is tender. Transfer the chicken to a serving dish, trimming the leg bones with poultry shears or a knife to neaten them, and keep it warm.

Add the stock to the pan and simmer the sauce uncovered until it is thick and concentrated, about 5 minutes, and then if the garlic is not soft, cook it for 5–10 minutes longer. Work the sauce through a sieve, pressing hard to extract the purée from the garlic. The chicken, and sauce, can be kept for up to three days in the refrigerator, or can be frozen. If you are doing this, reheat the chicken in the sauce if necessary and taste it for seasoning. Take it from the heat and arrange the chicken pieces on a serving dish.

To finish, whisk the remaining butter into the sauce in small pieces, taste it for seasoning and spoon it over the chicken. Sprinkle the dish with chopped parsley and serve at once.

CAILLES AUX PETITS POIS

Quail with green peas

Serves 6

Preparation and cooking time: 1 hour

6 large or 12 small quail
6–12 slices of streaky bacon
1 tablespoon vegetable oil
50 g (2 oz) unsalted butter
250 ml (8 fl oz) white wine
600 ml (1 pint) veal or chicken stock
750 g (1½ lb) shelled fresh or frozen and thawed peas
20–24 baby onions, peeled
1 teaspoon caster sugar
a few sprigs of fresh savory, marjoram or oregano or 2 teaspoons dried
beurre manié made with 25 g (1 oz) unsalted butter and 20 g (¾ oz) flour (page 8)
250 ml (8 fl oz) crème fraîche (page 7) or double cream
salt and pepper

Cailles aux Petits Pois

Often cooked with grapes like the pheasant on page 55, quail are also delicious with green peas.

Sprinkle the quail with salt and pepper, wrap them in bacon and tie them with string. Heat the oil and half the butter in a casserole and brown the birds well on all sides. Discard the fat from the pan and add the wine and 475 ml (16 fl oz) stock. Bring them to the boil, cover the pan and simmer for 20–25 minutes until the birds are tender.

Meanwhile braise the peas. Boil fresh peas in salted water until they are almost tender, the cooking time can vary from 10–20 minutes

*Coquelet en Crapaudine,
Sauce Moutarde
aux Champignons*

depending on their age. Drain them, rinse them with cold water and drain them again thoroughly; frozen peas need only be thawed. Melt the remaining butter in a pan, add the onions and sprinkle them with sugar. Cook them gently for 10–15 minutes until tender, shaking the pan so they brown evenly. Add the peas, remaining stock and the herbs with a little salt and pepper. Cover and simmer for 8–10 minutes until the peas are tender.

When the quail are cooked, discard the trussing strings and keep the birds warm. Bring the cooking liquid from the quail to the boil and whisk in the *beurre manié* a piece at a time until the sauce lightly coats a spoon. Stir in the *crème fraîche* or cream, bring back to the boil and taste the sauce for seasoning. Put the peas on a serving dish and set the quail on top. Spoon a little sauce over the quail and serve the rest separately.

Poulet Sauté au Vinaigre de Vin

COQUELET EN CRAPAUDINE, SAUCE MOUTARDE AUX CHAMPIGNONS

Grilled poussins with mustard and mushroom sauce   Serves 4

Preparation and cooking time: 1 hour

For the sauce:

25 g (1 oz) unsalted butter

150 g (5 oz) mushrooms, sliced

2 shallots, chopped finely

1 clove of garlic, chopped finely

4 tablespoons white wine

4 tablespoons white wine vinegar

1½ tablespoons Dijon mustard, or to taste

350 ml (12 fl oz) chicken stock

beurre manié made with 15 g (½ oz) flour and 20 g (¾ oz) butter (page 8)

To cook the poussins:

2 poussins or small chickens weighing about 750 g (1½ lb) each

25 g (1 oz) unsalted butter, melted

1 tablespoon Dijon mustard

2 tablespoons dried breadcrumbs

salt and pepper

To garnish:

a bunch of watercress

A 'crapaud' is a toad, which these small chickens are held to resemble after they have been flattened on skewers for grilling. The coating of Dijon mustard adds the Burgundian touch.

To make the sauce, melt half the butter in a pan and cook the mushrooms until tender and lightly browned. Melt the remaining butter in another pan and cook the shallots and garlic until they soften. Add the wine and vinegar and simmer until they have reduced to about 2 tablespoons. Stir in the mustard, add the stock and the mushrooms and simmer for about 5 minutes. Whisk in the kneaded butter a small piece at a time, until the sauce lightly coats the back of a spoon. Season with salt and pepper to taste. The sauce can be kept in the refrigerator for up to three days.

To cook the chickens, first heat the grill. Put one chicken on the work surface, breast-side down. Cut along each side of the backbone with poultry shears or a heavy knife and remove it. Snip the wishbone in half and turn the chicken breast-side up. With a sharp downward movement of the heel of the hand, press the chicken flat, breaking the breastbone. Skewer the chicken crossways, once through both the wings and again through the legs to hold it flat. Repeat this process with the other bird. Brush the chickens with melted butter and sprinkle them with salt and pepper.

Put the chickens on the grill rack, skin towards the heat, and cook them about 7.5 cm (3 inches) from the heat for 15 minutes, brushing them once during the grilling with butter. Turn them, brush them with the remaining butter and grill them for 10 minutes on the other side. Turn the chickens again skin-side up, brush them with the mustard and sprinkle them with the breadcrumbs. Grill until the birds are tender and browned, about 10 minutes longer. Watch them carefully and if they brown too quickly at any point during cooking, set the grill rack further from the heat.

To finish, reheat the sauce if necessary. Remove the skewers and cut the chickens in half at the breastbone. Arrange them on a serving dish or individual plates and garnish them with watercress. Spoon over a little sauce and serve the rest of the sauce separately.

FAISAN À LA VIGNERONNE

Pheasant with red and green grapes   Serves 4

Preparation and cooking time: 1 hour

2 pheasants weighing about 750 g (1½ lb) each, with giblets

2 thin slices of pork fat or 4 slices streaky bacon

65 g (2½ oz) unsalted butter

1 teaspoon marc or brandy

8 triangular fried bread croûtes (page 8)

For the sauce:

175 g (6 oz) seedless green grapes

175 g (6 oz) seedless red grapes

250 ml (8 fl oz) Chablis or dry white wine

3 tablespoons marc or brandy

250 ml (8 fl oz) veal or chicken stock

2 teaspoons arrowroot mixed to a paste with 2 tablespoons water

The French are fussy about game birds, distinguishing between old and young and cock and hen; the female, they say with a wink, is always to be preferred. In this recipe old birds will take at least an hour or even two to cook until they are tender. When pheasants are farm-raised, however, their tenderness is guaranteed and they can be cooked just until rare. Partridge, wild duck or guinea-fowl can be substituted for pheasant. If you use seedless grapes you'll avoid the tiresome job of scooping out the seeds.

Preheat the oven. Sprinkle the birds inside with salt and pepper and truss them. Cover the breasts with fat or bacon and tie it on with string. Heat 40 g (1½ oz) butter in a flameproof casserole and brown the pheasants thoroughly on all sides, taking 8–10 minutes. Add the giblets, including the liver, and cover the casserole. Cook in the oven for 25–30 minutes until the juices from the centre run pink but not red. If you prefer the birds well done, or if they are tough, continue cooking until the juice runs clear and they are tender when pierced with a skewer.

After 10 minutes, remove the pheasant liver from the casserole and crush it with the remaining butter, using a fork. Season it with

salt and pepper

To garnish:

a bunch of watercress
(optional)

Oven temperature:
Gas Mark 6/200°C/400°F

the teaspoon of marc or brandy, salt and pepper and spread it on the croûtes. Put the grapes in a pan with the wine and simmer them for 3–5 minutes until they are lightly cooked but not soft.

When the pheasants are cooked, pour off any excess fat, add the 3 tablespoons marc or brandy to the pan and flame it. Remove the pheasants from the pot, discard the fat or bacon and remove the trussing strings. With poultry shears or a heavy knife cut along each side of the backbone and remove it. Trim the leg bones to neaten them and cut the birds in half along the breastbone. Keep them warm.

Add the wine from cooking the grapes to the pot and boil it for about 2 minutes, stirring to dissolve the pan juices. Add the stock, bring it to the boil and strain the sauce. If the pheasant is well done, it can be stored for up to two days in the refrigerator with the sauce, keeping the garnish separate. If you like the bird rare, however, it should be cooked at the last minute and served immediately.

To finish, if necessary reheat the pheasants in the sauce on top of the stove, adding more stock if necessary to keep them moist. Arrange the pheasant pieces on a serving dish so they overlap and keep them warm. Mix the arrowroot paste if it has separated and whisk enough into the boiling sauce so it lightly coats a spoon. Add the grapes to the sauce, bring it just to the boil and spoon the sauce over the pheasant. Garnish the dish with croûtes and watercress if you like. Fried matchstick potatoes are the traditional accompaniment to this recipe.

Faisan à la Vigneronne

POULARDE AU VIN NUITONNE

Chicken in red wine sauce   Serves 6

Preparation time: 8 hours marinating + 50 minutes + 1½ hours cooking

For the marinade:

a bottle of well aged red burgundy

1 onion, sliced thinly

1 carrot, sliced thinly

1 stick of celery, sliced thinly

a bouquet garni

1 clove of garlic, sliced

1 teaspoon black peppercorns

2 tablespoons olive oil

To cook the chicken:

2.25 kg (5 lb) casserole hen or roasting chicken, cut into 8 pieces (page 46)

1 tablespoon vegetable oil

25 g (1 oz) butter

30 g (1¼ oz) flour

475 ml (16 fl oz) chicken or veal stock, or more if needed

2 cloves of garlic, crushed

2 shallots, chopped finely

salt and pepper

For the garnish:

1 tablespoon vegetable oil

25 g (1 oz) unsalted butter

175 g (6 oz) streaky bacon, cut in lardons (thin strips) and blanched if salty (page 31)

20–25 baby onions, peeled

250 g (8 oz) mushrooms, quartered

This dish should take at least three days, to allow time for the meat to marinate and then for the cooked bird to mellow in the wine sauce. To be faithful to the recipe title, you should use a wine from the Côtes de Nuits. The older the bird the better, whether cock or casserole hen ('poularde'); a large chicken is good too.

First prepare the marinade. In a pan (not an aluminium one which would mar the flavour) combine the wine, onion, carrot, celery, bouquet garni, garlic, peppercorns and olive oil. Bring the marinade to the boil, simmer it for 5 minutes and then leave it to cool completely. Put the chicken pieces in a deep bowl, pour over the marinade, cover and leave at room temperature for 8 hours or in the refrigerator for 10–12 hours, turning the pieces occasionally. Drain and dry the pieces of chicken. Strain the marinade and reserve both the liquid and the vegetables. Preheat the oven.

Heat the oil and butter in a casserole, add the pieces of chicken, skin-side down, and cook them over a medium heat until they are brown. Turn them to brown the other side, taking 10–15 minutes altogether. Take out the chicken and pour off all but about a tablespoon of fat. Add the vegetables from the marinade, saving the bouquet garni to add later, and cook gently until soft but not browned. Add the flour and cook, stirring, until foaming. Stir in the reserved marinade and bouquet garni, stock, garlic, shallots and salt and pepper. Replace the pieces of chicken, cover the casserole and bring it to the boil. Cook in the oven until the chicken is very tender and almost falling from the bone. For a boiling fowl this may take up to 1½ hours, but a roasting chicken will take only ¾–1 hour.

Meanwhile, prepare the garnish. Heat the oil and butter in a pan and fry the bacon until it is

1 tablespoon chopped parsley

Oven temperature:
Gas Mark 3/170°C/325°F

well browned and the fat is extracted; then remove it from the pan to drain. Put the onions in the pan and fry them gently until they are lightly browned and tender, about 10 minutes; shake the pan occasionally so that they colour evenly. Drain the onions and add them to the bacon. Finally fry the mushrooms for 4–5 minutes until they are brown and tender. Drain them and add them to the bacon as well.

When the chicken is cooked, remove the pieces and trim the thigh and leg joints to neaten them with poultry shears or a knife. Remove the bouquet garni. The sauce should be thick enough to coat a spoon lightly, so reduce it if necessary. Taste the sauce and then strain it over the garnish. Wipe out the casserole, replace the pieces of chicken and pour over the garnish and sauce. The chicken is best prepared at least a day ahead. It can be refrigerated for three days, or frozen.

Reheat the chicken on top of the stove. Serve it in the casserole, sprinkled with chopped parsley. Small fried potatoes or fried croûtes are the classic accompaniment.

MEAT

In Burgundy it is the everyday meat dishes which are so good: chops baked in cream sauce with mustard; rabbit in a pot with fresh thyme. Burgundians are particularly proud of their beef, which comes from the giant buff Charollais cattle which are bred in the gentle hills west of the Côte d'Or. Charollais beef is lean and makes indifferent roasts and steaks, but is ideal for the finest wine ragoûts whose fame has spread far beyond the province. 'What is this masterpiece?' demands a character in one of the novels of Colette. 'It's beef.' 'But there is in this dish a mystery, a magic. One should be able to put a name to such a marvel.' 'To be sure,' replied Madam Yvon, 'it's beef.'

Tourte Bourguignonne

*Boeuf Bourguignon
à l'Ancienne*

*Lapin au Thym
Chef Chambrette*

BOEUF BOURGUIGNON À L'ANCIENNE

Preparation time: 50 minutes + 4¼ hours cooking   Serves 8

3 tablespoons vegetable oil

1.75 g (4 lb) stewing or braising beef, cut in 5 cm (2-inch) cubes

1 onion, sliced

1 carrot, sliced

20 g (¾ oz) plain flour

a bottle of red burgundy

250 ml (8 fl oz) beef stock, or more if needed

2 cloves of garlic, chopped

a bouquet garni

salt and pepper

For the garnish:

1 tablespoon vegetable oil

300 g (10 oz) streaky bacon, cut in lardons (thin strips) and blanched if salty (page 31)

25–30 baby onions, peeled

300 g (10 oz) mushrooms, quartered

8 heart-shaped or triangular fried bread croûtes (page 8)

2 tablespoons chopped parsley

Oven temperature:
Gas Mark 3/170°C/325°F

When he makes a 'bourguignon', Chef Chambrette roams the market like a hunter, seeking out just the right pieces of lean, dark meat with plenty of connective tissue to dissolve during cooking and enrich the sauce. In Britain a good cut to choose would be chuck steak. I've also cooked oxtail 'à la bourguignonne': it takes about five hours and a wonderfully rich sauce results. Whichever meat you use, the secret of a really good flavour is to take the time to brown the ingredients thoroughly.

Preheat the oven. Heat two tablespoons of the oil in a heavy casserole and brown the beef very thoroughly on all sides, a few pieces at a time. Use a high heat and allow 8–10 minutes for each batch. Take out the meat.

Add the remaining oil, sliced onion and the carrot to the casserole and cook until the vegetables are very brown. Add the flour and cook, stirring, for 1–2 minutes. Pour in the wine and stock, add the garlic, bouquet garni, salt and pepper and replace the beef. Cover the casserole, bring it to the boil and cook it in the oven for 3–4 hours or until the beef is very tender. Stir the casserole from time to time during cooking and add more stock if it gets dry.

To prepare the garnish, heat the oil and fry the bacon until it is well browned and set it aside. Add the onions, brown them and add them to the bacon. Finally fry the mushrooms until they are tender and add them to the onions and bacon.

When it is cooked, transfer the beef to another casserole, which will be used for serving. The sauce should be dark and rich but if it seems thin, boil and reduce it. Taste it for seasoning and strain it over the beef. Stir in the garnish of bacon, onion and mushrooms, cover and continue cooking in the oven for 10–15 minutes until the onions are tender. Boeuf bourguignon can be kept for up to three days in the refrigerator and the flavour mellows with keeping.

If necessary, reheat the beef on top of the stove. Dip each croûte in the sauce and then in the chopped parsley and arrange them around the edge of the casserole. Sprinkle the beef with the remaining parsley. Small boiled or fried potatoes are the classic accompaniment, but I prefer a green vegetable such as beans or broccoli.

RAGOÛT DE PORC AUX POIREAUX

Pork stew with leeks   Serves 6

Preparation time: 30 minutes + 50 minutes cooking

1 kg (2 lb) boned pork loin

3 tablespoons olive oil

2 cloves of garlic, chopped finely

250 ml (8 fl oz) full-bodied white wine

500 g (1 lb) tomatoes, peeled, de-seeded and chopped

1 kg (2 lb) leeks

1 tablespoon chopped parsley

salt and pepper

Oven temperature:
Gas Mark 4/180°C/350°F

Monsieur Milbert's leeks are monumental: great giants the size of a small rolling pin. I have to confess they are not my favourite vegetable, though they are remarkably well disguised in this simple pork stew from 'La Vieille Cuisine Bourguignonne' printed in Dijon in 1936. 'For the preparation of this excellent dish,' remarks the author, 'it is essential to use very good olive oil.'

Preheat the oven. Cut the pork into six thick steaks, discarding any string, and sprinkle them with salt and pepper. Heat the oil in a flameproof casserole with the garlic. Add the pork steaks and brown them thoroughly, allowing 4–5 minutes on each side. Add the wine and tomatoes, cover and simmer for 15 minutes. Meanwhile, trim the leeks, leaving some green top. Split them, wash them very well and slice them.

Take the pork steaks from the casserole, add the leeks with salt and pepper and stir to mix. Cover the casserole and cook gently for 5 minutes. Place the pork on top of the leeks, cover and cook in the oven for 40–50 minutes until the pork is very tender. The ragoût can be kept for up to three days in the refrigerator. Reheat it gently on top of the stove and serve it in the casserole, sprinkled with chopped parsley.

CÔTES DE VEAU DIJONNAISE

Veal chops with mustard sauce   Serves 4

Preparation time: 50 minutes + 30 minutes cooking

125 g (4 oz) streaky bacon, cut in lardons (thin strips) and blanched if salty (page 31)

1 tablespoon vegetable oil

25 g (1 oz) unsalted butter

4 large veal chops

1 tablespoon plain flour

175 ml (6 fl oz) white wine

175 ml (6 fl oz) veal stock

a bouquet garni

4 tablespoons crème fraîche (page 7) or double cream

1 tablespoon Dijon mustard, or to taste

1 tablespoon chopped parsley

salt and pepper

Oven temperature (optional):
Gas Mark 4/180°C/350°F

Fine mustard is associated with wine-growing areas because 'ver jus', or acid grape juice, is one of its essential ingredients. The Burgundian taste for mustard goes back a long way and the medieval Dukes of Burgundy, with their capital at Dijon, would present their guests with a barrel of mustard to take home. The following recipe is equally good made with pork chops.

Preheat the oven if you are using it. Fry the bacon in the oil in a sauté pan or deep frying pan until browned and then drain it on paper towels. Discard all but a tablespoon of the fat from the pan and add the butter. Season the chops with salt and pepper and fry them for 2–3 minutes on each side until browned. Take them out, add the flour and cook until it is foaming. Whisk in the wine, stock, bouquet garni, salt and pepper and bring the sauce to the boil, whisking constantly. Replace the chops and bacon in the sauce, cover and simmer on top of the stove or in the oven for 40–50 minutes until the chops are tender. They can be cooked up to three days ahead and refrigerated.

To finish: reheat the chops in the sauce on top of the stove if necessary and then transfer them to a serving dish and keep them warm. Add the *crème fraîche* or cream to the sauce and bring it just back to the boil. Take it from the heat, whisk in the mustard and taste, adding more if necessary. Discard the bouquet garni, spoon the sauce over the chops, and sprinkle them with chopped parsley.

Ragoût de Porc aux Poireaux
Côtes de Veau Dijonnaise

TOURTE BOURGUIGNONNE

Pork and veal pie with cream   Serves 6–8

Preparation time: 1 hour + 15 minutes chilling
+ 1 hour 15 minutes baking

*pâte brisée made with 375 g
(12 oz) plain flour, 175 g
(6 oz) unsalted butter, 1 egg,
1 teaspoon salt and
4 tablespoons cold water, or
more if needed (page 8)*

For the filling:

*500 g (1 lb) pork shoulder,
without bone*

*500 g (1 lb) veal shoulder,
without bone*

3 shallots, chopped finely

*25 g (1 oz) unsalted butter,
plus extra for greasing*

*125 ml (4 fl oz) dry white
burgundy*

*1 tablespoon salt, or more if
needed*

*1 teaspoon ground black
pepper*

1 teaspoon ground allspice

*2 tablespoons chopped
parsley*

4 eggs

*475 ml (16 fl oz) crème
fraîche (page 7) or double
cream*

To glaze:

*1 egg beaten with
½ teaspoon salt*

Oven temperatures:
*Gas Mark 6/200°C/400°F
Gas Mark 4/180°C/350°F*

*The word 'tourte' always catches my eye, for it
implies just my kind of hearty country cooking. A
tourte is usually baked in a deep mould with a top and
a bottom crust and in this version it is filled with a veal
and pork stuffing enriched with eggs and cream. The
recipe is adapted from 'Les Recettes de la Table
Bourguignonne', a handy compendium dedicated to
'Burgundians and all lovers of regional cooking'. This
tourte is good hot or cold.*

Grease a 25 cm (10-inch) diameter, deep quiche
mould or spring-form cake tin. Roll two-thirds
of the dough into a 33 cm (13-inch) circle, roll it
around the rolling pin and then unroll it over the
tin. Gently lift the dough and press it into the
corners of the tin and up the sides; trim the
edges, leaving a small overlap. Chill the pastry.

To make the filling, trim any fat and sinew
from the pork and veal and work them through
the fine blade of a mincer. Fry the shallots in the
butter until soft. Add the wine and simmer until
it has reduced by about half and then beat it into
the meat with the salt, pepper, allspice and
parsley. Fry a small piece of the filling and taste
it: it should be quite spicy so if necessary add
more seasoning. Whisk the eggs with the *crème
fraîche* or cream until they are thoroughly mixed.

Roll half the filling into balls the size of an egg
and set them in the pastry shell, leaving space
between them. Pour over some of the cream
mixture until it is level with the meat. Roll the
remaining meat into balls, put them on top of
the first layer and pour over the remaining cream
mixture.

Brush the edges of the pastry shell with the
egg glaze. Roll the remaining dough to a 25 cm
(10-inch) circle and lift it on to the meat with the
rolling pin. Trim the edges of the dough, press

them together and flute them to seal. With the point of a knife, make 2–3 holes in the centre of the tourte to allow steam to escape and decorate the top with leaves made with pastry trimmings. Brush the top with egg glaze. Chill the tourte for 15 minutes or until the dough is firm and preheat the oven to the higher setting.

Brush the tourte again with glaze and bake it in the oven for 20 minutes or until it is starting to brown. Lower the heat to the second setting and continue baking for 45–55 minutes or until a skewer inserted in the centre of the tourte is hot to the touch when withdrawn after 30 seconds. If the top starts to brown too much during baking, cover it loosely with foil. The tourte can be kept for up to three days in the refrigerator. Serve it warm or at room temperature but do not cut it while it is very hot.

LAPIN AU THYM CHEF CHAMBRETTE

Rabbit with thyme en cocotte   Serves 4

Preparation time: 20 minutes + 3½ hours cooking

250 g (8 oz) slices of streaky bacon, blanched if salty

2 onions, sliced thickly

a large bunch of fresh thyme

1.5 kg (3 lb) rabbit joints

300 ml (½ pint) full-bodied white burgundy

600 ml (1 pint) veal or chicken stock, or more if needed

salt and pepper

Oven temperature:
Gas Mark 3/160°C/325°F

I shall never forget the day Chef Chambrette pursued Madame Milbert down the garden path waving a bunch of thyme and shouting 'You call that a basketfull! Give me more!' He used almost all of it in cooking a couple of rabbits and then presented her with one as a peace offering. The rabbit can be served hot or try it cold, when the cooking juices set to a light aspic.

Preheat the oven. Lay half the bacon slices in the base of a 3.75-litre (6-pint) terrine or casserole and cover them with about a third of the onion slices and a sprig or two of thyme. Add half the rabbit, sprinkling the pieces with salt and pepper. Top with more onions and thyme and then add the rest of the rabbit with salt, pepper and the remaining thyme, onion and bacon. Press the ingredients down well and pour over the wine with enough stock to cover. Cover the terrine tightly and cook it in the oven for 3–3½ hours until the rabbit is very tender, if necessary adding more stock during cooking to keep the rabbit covered in liquid.

Let the terrine cool slightly and then lift out the pieces of rabbit, the onion and bacon. Strain the cooking broth, discarding the thyme sprigs, and boil it if necessary until reduced to about 600 ml (1 pint). Replace the rabbit, bacon and onions in the terrine and pour over the broth. The rabbit can be kept for up to three days in the refrigerator. If you are serving it cold, try it with a potato vinaigrette; if hot, boiled rice is a good accompaniment.

RAGOÛT DE CHEVREUIL DU FEŸ

Venison stew with wild mushrooms   Serves 6

Preparation time: 2–3 days marinating + 25 minutes + 2½ hours cooking

1.5 kg (3 lb) boned loin or haunch of venison, cut in 5 cm (2-inch) cubes
30 g (1¼ oz) unsalted butter
1 tablespoon vegetable oil
30 g (1¼ oz) plain flour
250 ml (8 fl oz) dark stock, or more if needed
30 g (1¼ oz) dried girolles, cèpes (boletus) or other wild mushrooms
250 ml (8 fl oz) crème fraîche (page 7) or double cream
6–12 round or triangular fried bread croûtes (page 8)
salt and pepper
For the marinade:
a bottle of full-bodied red burgundy
2 onions, quartered
4 shallots, halved

One memorable autumn, thanks to a happy coincidence of warmth and rain, our nearby woods were filled with spindly grey 'trumpet of death' mushrooms. Far from living up to their name, they are very edible and we dried strings of them to use in dishes like this stew. Deer occasionally appear in the woods too, though they do not long survive the local poachers. This could also be made with beef or lamb.

First make the marinade. Mix the wine, vegetables and bouquet garni in a deep bowl (not an aluminium one). Add the venison, mix well and spoon the oil over the top. Cover the bowl and leave the meat to marinate for 2–3 days in the refrigerator.

Preheat the oven. Drain the meat, reserving the marinade and vegetables, and pat it dry with paper towels. Heat the butter and oil in a heavy casserole and brown the meat thoroughly on all sides, a few pieces at a time. Remove the meat, add the vegetables from the marinade and cook, stirring, until they are browned. Add the flour and cook for 1 minute. Stir in the marinade, stock, salt and pepper, replace the meat and

Ragoût de Chevreuil du Feÿ

3 cloves of garlic, chopped

1 leek, split and sliced

2 carrots, sliced

a bouquet garni

2 tablespoons vegetable oil

Oven temperature:
Gas Mark 4/180°C/350°F

bring the ragoût to the boil. Cook it in the oven until the venison is very tender, stirring it occasionally and adding more stock if it gets dry. If the venison is young, 1½–2 hours cooking should suffice, but older meat may take much longer, about 2–3 hours.

Pour boiling water over the mushrooms and leave them to soak for half an hour. Drain and rinse them thoroughly to remove any sand. When the venison is tender, remove it and strain the sauce. Add the mushrooms to the sauce and simmer them for 15–20 minutes or until the mushrooms are tender and the sauce is thick enough to coat a spoon lightly. Add the *crème fraîche* or cream, simmer for 5 minutes longer and taste for seasoning. Replace the meat in the sauce. The ragoût can be kept in the refrigerator for up to three days and the flavour mellows with keeping.

To finish: reheat the ragoût on top of the stove if necessary. Transfer it to a serving dish and arrange the croûtes on top or around the edge. Soufflé de Marrons (Chestnut soufflé, page 71) is a good accompaniment, together with noodles.

VEGETABLES AND SALADS

When planning this chapter, I hardly knew where to begin. Potatoes alone offer so many possibilities, not to mention all the greens that grow so well in the benign Burgundian climate. Green beans and kidney beans flourish, as do vines like cucumber, courgette and pumpkin, while the onion family, including leeks and garlic, is practically synonymous with Burgundian cuisine. So this is a very personal choice of what I particularly enjoy.

In rural France vegetables often act as an appetiser and all the following recipes could open a meal rather than accompany the main course.

SOUFFLÉ DE MARRONS

Chestnut soufflé   Serves 6–8

Preparation time: 20 minutes + 20 minutes baking

500 g (1 lb) fresh chestnuts or canned unsweetened chestnuts

300 ml (½ pint) crème fraîche (page 7) or double cream

1 teaspoon ground allspice

½ teaspoon ground nutmeg

½ teaspoon ground cloves

4 egg yolks

butter for greasing

6 egg whites

40 g (1½ oz) walnuts

salt and pepper

Oven temperature:
Gas Mark 5/190°C/375°F

The avenue of chestnut trees leading from our gate is marked on a map of 1751. In those days, chestnuts, cooked in soup or ground to flour and baked in unleavened cakes, often took the place of grain in years of bad harvest. Chestnut soufflé is particularly good with game and roast poultry.

Unless you are preparing the chestnut mixture in advance, preheat the oven. If you are using fresh chestnuts, pierce each nut with the point of a knife. Put them in cold water and bring to the boil. Drain a few at a time and peel them while they are still hot, removing both the outer and inner skins. If they are cool and become hard to peel, reheat them. If using canned chestnuts, just drain them; they do not need to be cooked.

Work the chestnuts through a sieve, put them in a saucepan and stir in the cream. The chestnuts can also be puréed with 2–3 tablespoons of the cream in a food processor. Heat the purée until it is very hot and add the allspice, nutmeg and cloves. Season with salt and pepper: the soufflé should be highly seasoned to compensate for the blandness of the egg whites. Take the pan from the heat and beat in the egg yolks which will cook and thicken the chestnut mixture slightly. This mixture can be prepared up to 8 hours ahead and kept in the refrigerator.

Butter a 3-litre (5½-pint) gratin or shallow baking dish. If necessary, warm the chestnut mixture until it is hot to touch. Stiffly whip the egg whites, adding a pinch of salt to help them stiffen. Add about a quarter of the whites to the chestnut mixture and stir gently until thoroughly combined: the heat of the mixture will cook the egg whites lightly and make them firm. Add this mixture to the remaining egg whites and fold the two together as lightly as possible. Spread the mixture in the gratin or baking dish, chop the walnuts and sprinkle them on top. Bake for 15–20 minutes until the soufflé is puffed up and brown. Serve it at once.

CRAPIAUX MORVANDIAUX

Grated potato pancakes   Serves 4

Preparation and cooking time: 30 minutes

500 g (1 lb) potatoes

2 eggs, beaten lightly

30 g (1¼ oz) plain flour

3–4 tablespoons milk

5–6 tablespoons vegetable oil

salt and pepper

This recipe comes from 'Les Secrets de la Mère Brazier'; Mère Brazier was one of the most famous women cooks of Lyon. Crapiaux can be eaten hot or cold, as a supper dish or as the accompaniment to chicken or meat with sauce. I sometimes add a few tablespoons of chopped ham to the batter, particularly if the pancakes are to be served on their own.

Peel the potatoes, coarsely grate them and at once mix them with the eggs so they do not

Petits Oignons en Confit
Haricots au Vin
Crapiaux Morvandiaux

discolour. Stir in the flour, salt, pepper, and enough milk to make a batter the consistency of double cream. The batter must be used at once as the potatoes discolour quickly.

Heat a tablespoon of oil in the frying pan and add enough batter to form a 5 mm (¼-inch) layer. Fry the pancake briskly for 2–3 minutes until brown; turn it and brown the other side. Fry the remaining batter in the same way, adding more oil as needed; this quantity will make 4–6 pancakes. Keep the finished pancakes warm in the oven as you work if they are to be served hot. They can be kept a few hours for serving cold.

HARICOTS AU VIN

Kidney beans with wine	Serves 4–6

Preparation time: soaking overnight + 15 minutes + 3 hours cooking

500 g (1 lb) dried kidney beans

1 onion, studded with 4 cloves

1 carrot

a bouquet garni

125 ml (4 fl oz) red or white wine

125 ml (4 fl oz) crème fraîche (page 7) or double cream (optional)

25 g (1 oz) unsalted butter

2 tablespoons chopped savory or parsley

salt and pepper

One of the treats of a French country market is the multi-coloured array of kidney beans, at their best in early autumn when fresh beans can be cooked without any preliminary soaking in cold water. In this versatile recipe I like to use red wine with red and purple beans and white wine with green and white ones.

Soak the beans overnight in cold water to cover and then drain them. Pick them over and put them in a saucepan with the onion, carrot, bouquet garni and enough water to cover everything generously. Bring to a brisk boil for 10 minutes and then cover the pan and let it simmer until the beans are very tender, adding water if necessary to keep them covered. Dried beans may take up to 3 hours; much depends on the type of bean.

Drain the beans and discard the onion, carrot and bouquet garni. Add the wine, and cream if you are using it, simmer the beans for 5–10 minutes longer and then taste. Add the butter in small pieces, shaking the pan so it melts into the sauce. The beans can be chilled for up to three days or frozen, and reheated. Sprinkle with savory or parsley just before serving.

PETITS OIGNONS EN CONFIT

Preserved baby onions   Serves 4–6

Preparation time: 5 minutes + 1¾ hours cooking

500 g (1 lb) baby onions, peeled

300 ml (½ pint) water

6 cloves of garlic, chopped coarsely

3 tablespoons each of red wine vinegar, olive oil, brown sugar, tomato purée and raisins

salt and pepper

Confit is a traditional method of preserving foods by long slow cooking until they are meltingly soft. Usually a confit is made with duck or goose, but vegetables can also be cooked 'en confit', rather like a chutney, to last through the winter. These onions are good with roast pork and duck, whether hot or cold.

Combine all the ingredients in a heavy pan and simmer them very gently, covered, for 1 hour. Remove the lid and continue cooking for 30–45 minutes more until most of the liquid has evaporated and the onions are glazed and very soft. Taste the confit for seasoning. It can be kept in the refrigerator for up to three months if sealed. Serve it hot or at room temperature.

SALADE AU LARD

Hot bacon salad   Serves 4

Preparation and cooking time: 10 minutes

a medium-size head of curly endive or escarole

2 tablespoons oil

125 g (4 oz) streaky bacon, cut in lardons (thin strips) and blanched if salty (page 31)

6 tablespoons wine vinegar

salt and pepper

Any robust greens such as curly endive or escarole can be used for this winter salad. In France dandelions are popular and you'll see enthusiasts combing the fields for wild ones, particularly just after the first frost when the jagged leaves are at their best.

Thoroughly wash the salad greens, drain and dry them. Put them in a salad bowl.

Heat the oil and fry the bacon until lightly browned but still tender. Discard the excess fat, leaving about 6 tablespoons. Pour the bacon and fat over the greens and toss well. The heat will wilt the leaves slightly. Add the vinegar to the hot pan, standing back from the fumes, and cook until it has reduced by half. Pour it over the salad and toss again. Taste it, adding pepper and salt if needed, and serve it at once.

POMMES DE TERRE LYONNAISE

Fried potatoes with onion   Serves 4

Preparation and cooking time: 40 minutes

750 g (1½ lb) potatoes

3 tablespoons vegetable oil

40 g (1½ oz) unsalted
butter

3 medium-size onions,
sliced thinly

1 tablespoon chopped
parsley

salt and pepper

*In classic French cuisine 'à la lyonnaise' means a dish
with onions. With any kind of grilled meat or poultry,
I find this combination of crisply browned potatoes and
dark, caramelised onions irresistible.*

Scrub the potatoes and put them, unpeeled, in a
saucepan of cold, salted water. Cover the pan,
bring it to the boil and simmer for 15–20 minutes
until the potatoes are nearly tender. Drain and
peel them while they are still warm and cut them
into 5 mm (¼-inch) slices.

Meanwhile, heat half the oil and butter in a
large frying pan and fry the onions over a
medium heat for 8–10 minutes or until they are
deep golden-brown. Lift them out with a
draining spoon. Fry the warm potatoes briskly
in the remaining oil and butter until they are
golden brown, tossing or turning them
occasionally with a spatula. The longer the
potatoes are fried, the crisper they will be. Add
the onions, salt and pepper, mix well and
continue cooking for 2–3 minutes so the
flavours blend; then sprinkle with parsley and
serve. The potatoes can be cooked a few hours
ahead and reheated, but they will not be so crisp.

*Salade au Lard
Pommes de Terre Lyonnaise*

GRATIN DE TOPINAMBOURS ET POMMES DE TERRE

Gratin of jerusalem artichokes and potatoes   Serves 6–8

Preparation time: 35 minutes + 25 minutes baking

1.25 litres (2¼ pints) milk

500 g (1 lb) jerusalem artichokes

500 g (1 lb) potatoes

1 clove of garlic, peeled

25 g (1 oz) unsalted butter

grated nutmeg

350 ml (12 fl oz) crème fraîche (page 7) or double cream

75 g (3 oz) grated Gruyère cheese

salt and pepper

Oven temperature:
Gas Mark 4/180°C/350°F

One year we planted a few jerusalem artichokes in the garden and we've had them ever since, for they are persistent and prolific plants. At La Varenne in Paris, the chefs are adept at turning a weekly crateful of roots into delicacies and this recipe, a version of potato 'gratin dauphinois' is one of their best inventions. Turnips can be substituted for the artichokes. A rich gratin like this is often served with roast or grilled beef.

Preheat the oven. Divide the milk between two pans, adding salt and pepper. Peel the artichokes, slice them thinly and add them at once to one milk pan, to prevent their discolouring. Bring them to a boil and simmer for 20–25 minutes until they are almost tender. Meanwhile, peel the potatoes, slice them thinly and add them quickly to the other pan of milk. Bring it to the boil and simmer until they are almost tender, 15–20 minutes.

Drain both vegetables, reserving a total of 350 ml (12 fl oz) of the milk and keeping the rest for another purpose such as soup. Rub a shallow baking dish with the garlic and then butter it. Put half the potatoes and jerusalem artichokes in the baking dish and season them with salt and pepper. Add the remaining vegetables and season again. Stir the nutmeg into the cream and pour it over the vegetables with the reserved milk. Sprinkle with the grated cheese. The gratin can be prepared up to 12 hours ahead and kept in the refrigerator. Bake the gratin for 25–30 minutes until it is very hot and the top has browned.

PASTRIES AND BREADS

All French cooks agree that the famous crusty French loaves are best left to an expert touch. Sweet breads, wholewheat, and the occasional batch of brioche are another matter, however. Pastry, too, is never so good as when freshly made at home with the best butter. It is here that really good ingredients count, and the mystique of grandmother's secrets passed down from hand to hand is never more important.

SAUCE AUX ABRICOTS

Apricot jam sauce   Makes 300 ml (½ pint)

Preparation time: 10 minutes

250 g (8 oz) apricot jam

250 ml (8 fl oz) water, or more if needed

juice of 1 orange or lemon

A sauce to serve hot or cold.

Melt the jam with the water and lemon juice until smooth and then sieve the mixture. Add more water if necessary to make a sauce which pours easily. It can be kept for a week in the refrigerator.

TARTE AUX POMMES LEGÈRE

Light apple tart   Serves 4

Preparation and cooking time: 1 hour + 1 hour chilling

pâte brisée made with 200 g (7 oz) plain flour, 90 g (3½ oz) unsalted butter, 40 g (1½ oz) caster sugar, 1 egg yolk, ½ teaspoon salt and 2 tablespoons cold water or more if needed (page 8)

4 tart cooking apples

60 g (2½ oz) unsalted butter, melted, plus extra for greasing

125 g (4 oz) caster sugar

Oven temperature:
Gas Mark 6/200°C/400°F

Tarte aux Pommes Legère

A speciality of the new-style chefs around Lyon, this wafer-thin apple tart bids fair to become a classic. Each person receives a spectacular wheel of apples arranged in concentric circles and glazed with caramelised sugar. As gilding to the lily, at the renowned Restaurant Lameloise in Chagny I was served an apple sherbet as an accompaniment.

Divide the dough into four, roll each piece into a 20 cm (8-inch) circle and transfer these to two buttered baking sheets. Trim the rounds with a knife using a pan lid as guide. Peel, core and slice the apples as thinly as possible. Starting at the outside edge, arrange the slices, rounded-side out, in concentric circles on the dough, overlapping the slices slightly. Take care that the

80

dough is completely covered, especially round the edges, so it does not scorch during baking. Brush the apples with melted butter and sprinkle each circle with a tablespoon of sugar. Cover the tarts with clingfilm and keep them in the refrigerator for at least 1 hour and for up to 8 hours.

Preheat the oven. Sprinkle each tart with another tablespoon of sugar and bake them for 7–10 minutes until the pastry is crisp. Preheat the grill to the highest heat and cook the tarts for 1–2 minutes until the apples are browned and caramelised. Serve them hot, with *crème fraîche* or vanilla ice cream if you like.

Corniottes Bourguignonnes

Bugnes

BUGNES

Preparation and cooking time: 35 minutes + 1½ hours chilling

1½ teaspoons baking powder

330 g (11 oz) plain flour, or more if needed, plus extra for kneading

45 g (1¾ oz) unsalted butter

3 eggs

½ teaspoon salt

45 g (1¾ oz) caster sugar

1 tablespoon light rum

grated rind of 1 orange or lemon

vegetable oil for deep-frying

icing sugar

Around Lyon, deep-fried bugnes, tied in a characteristic knot, are a favourite between-meal snack. For dessert I like to serve them with Sauce aux Abricots (Apricot jam sauce, page 79) or honey.

Sift the baking powder and three-quarters of the flour into a bowl and make a well in the centre. Pound the butter to soften it and put it in the well with the eggs, salt, sugar, rum and grated orange or lemon rind. Mix the ingredients in the well thoroughly and then stir in the flour. Knead the dough by pulling the mixture up and slapping it against the sides of the bowl. The dough will be very sticky at this point. Continue kneading in this manner, gradually working in the remaining flour. Turn on to a floured work surface and knead it for 2–3 minutes until it is very smooth, working in a little more flour if necessary. The dough can also be made and kneaded in an electric mixer using the dough hook. Shape it into a ball, wrap it and chill it for half an hour.

Roll out the dough as thinly as possible, trim the edges, and cut the dough lengthways into strips about 15 cm (6 inches) wide with a fluted ravioli wheel cutter or a knife. Cut each strip into 6.5 cm (2½-inch) diamonds; this quantity makes about 40. Cut a lengthwise slit in the centre of each diamond and pull one longer corner through the slit to form a knot. Set the bugnes on a floured tray; cover them and keep them chilled for at least an hour. They can be prepared up to 24 hours ahead.

Heat the deep fat to 190°C/375°F. Add several bugnes; the fat should be hot enough to make them rise at once to the surface. Fry them about 2 minutes until they are brown on one side and then turn them over and brown the other. Drain them on paper towels and keep them warm in a low oven with the door open while you fry the rest. Sprinkle the bugnes with icing sugar and serve them at once with the apricot jam sauce or honey in a separate bowl.

CORNIOTTES BOURGUIGNONNES

Fruit pastries   Makes 8

Preparation time: 25 minutes + 15 minutes chilling + 25 minutes baking

butter for greasing

750 g (1½ lb) apricots, greengages, damsons or bilberries

pâte brisée made with 200 g (7 oz) plain flour, 90 g (3½ oz) unsalted butter, 1 tablespoon caster sugar, 1 egg yolk, ½ teaspoon salt and 2 tablespoons cold water or more if needed (page 8)

5–6 tablespoons caster sugar

1 egg, beaten lightly with ½ teaspoon salt

125 ml (4 fl oz) double cream

a few drops of vanilla essence

Oven temperature:
Gas Mark 5/190°C/375°F

Always triangle-shaped, corniottes can be filled with cheese as well as with fruit. During the vendange (wine harvest) a giant version, as large as can be crammed into the oven, is sometimes made.

Preheat the oven and butter a baking sheet. Halve the stone fruit, leaving the skin and discarding the stones; pick over bilberries.

Roll out the pastry dough to about 5 mm (¼-inch) thick and stamp out eight rounds with a 13 cm (5-inch) pastry cutter. Mix the fruit with sugar to taste, reserving a tablespoon of sugar, and put a large spoonful of fruit in the centre of each round. Brush the edges of the dough with the beaten egg and fold them in from three directions to form a triangle that nearly encloses the fruit. Pinch the angles to seal them and turn them up slightly so no juice runs out during baking. Set the pastries on the prepared baking sheet and chill them for 15 minutes.

Brush the pastries with the remaining egg glaze and bake them in the oven for 20–25 minutes until they are brown and the fruit is cooked. They can be baked ahead and kept for a day or two in an airtight container: warm in a low oven before serving.

Whip the cream to soft peaks, add the remaining tablespoon of sugar and vanilla essence and continue whipping until the cream is stiff. Set a spoonful of cream on top of each hot pastry and serve them at once.

PAIN AUX NOIX

Walnut bread   Makes 2 loaves
(Pictured on page 4)

Preparation time: 30 minutes + 2½ hours rising + 45 minutes baking

400 g (13 oz) wholemeal flour, or more if needed, plus extra for kneading

125 g (4 oz) plain flour

2½ teaspoons salt

475 ml (16 fl oz) lukewarm water

1 tablespoon clear honey

7 g (¼ oz) dried yeast

oil and butter for greasing

150 g (5 oz) walnut halves, broken in half

Oven temperatures:
Gas Mark 7/220°C/425°F
Gas Mark 5/190°C/375°F

Just outside our gate stands an ancient walnut tree. Despite its size, the supply of nuts is meagre and they tend to be reserved for treats like this chewy wholemeal bread.

Put both types of flour with the salt on a work surface. Make a well in the centre and pour in a quarter of the water. Add the honey and then sprinkle the yeast on top and leave it for 5 minutes or until dissolved. Add the remaining water and work with your fingertips, gradually drawing in the flour to make large crumbs. Press them together to form a ball of dough which should be soft and quite sticky.

Sprinkle the work surface with flour and knead the dough for 5–10 minutes, working in more flour as necessary until it is smooth and elastic. The dough can also be mixed and kneaded in an electric mixer using the dough hook. Put the dough in a lightly oiled bowl, turn it over so the top is oiled and cover with a damp cloth. Leave it to rise in a warm place for 1–1½ hours or until it has doubled in bulk. Butter two 18 cm (7-inch) round cake tins.

Knead the risen dough lightly to knock out the air and then work in the walnuts. Divide the dough in half and shape it into rounds on a floured board. Set them in the tins, cover them with a damp cloth and leave to rise again in a warm place for 1 hour, or until doubled in size. Meanwhile, preheat the oven to the higher setting.

Sprinkle the breads lightly with wholemeal flour and slash the top of each loaf three or four times with a knife. Bake them in the oven for 15 minutes. Lower the heat to the second setting and continue baking for another 30–40 minutes or until the loaves sound hollow when tapped on the bottom. Turn them out on to a rack to cool.

After a day or two in an airtight container, the loaves will be firmer but still good, and they keep perfectly in the freezer.

PAIN D'ÉPICE

Spice bread   Makes a large loaf

Preparation time: 45 minutes + 55 minutes baking

150 ml (¼ pint) hot water

100 g (3½ oz) caster sugar

200 g (7 oz) honey

butter for greasing

200 g (7 oz) rye flour

90 g (3½ oz) plain flour

1 egg yolk

grated zest of 1 orange

1 teaspoon baking powder

¼ teaspoon ground mixed spice

¼ teaspoon ground cloves

¼ teaspoon ground cinnamon

For the icing:

1 egg white

75 g (3 oz) icing sugar, or more if needed

Oven temperature:
Gas Mark 4/180°C/350°F

At the height of the power of the Dukes of Burgundy, when spices were imported from the East through Flanders, spice bread was known as 'gâteau ducal' (the Duke's cake). It still forms one of the 'trois glorieuses' (three glories) of Dijon, together with mustard and cassis liqueur. Small cakes of spice bread are called 'nonettes' after the 'little nuns' who often used to bake them.

Put the water, sugar and honey in a saucepan and bring it to the boil, stirring. Leave to cool to tepid. Preheat the oven. Butter a 10 × 12 × 23 cm (4 × 5 × 9-inch) loaf tin, line it with paper and butter the paper as well.

For the batter, stir both kinds of flour together in a large bowl and make a well in the centre. Put three-quarters of the melted honey mixture with the egg yolk into the well and stir, gradually drawing in the flour to make a smooth, stiff batter. In a small bowl mix the orange zest, baking powder and spices; stir in the remaining honey, and stir this mixture into the batter.

Spoon the batter into the prepared tin, smoothing the top with the back of a wet spoon. Bake it in the oven for 45–55 minutes or until the bread shrinks slightly from the sides of the pan and a skewer inserted in the centre comes out clean. Leave it in the tin.

For the icing: using a wooden spoon, beat the egg white and icing sugar in a small bowl until they are very smooth and white. The icing should lightly coat the back of the spoon but if it is too thin, beat in more sugar. Unmould the bread and, while still warm, pour over the icing so it coats the loaf and drips slightly down the sides.

GALETTE VIEUX PÉROUGES

Yeast cake with lemon and sugar   Serves 6–8

Preparation time: 30 minutes + 1¾ hours rising
+ 20–25 minutes cooking

---

7 g (¼ oz) dried yeast

175 ml (6 fl oz) lukewarm water

350 g (12 oz) plain flour, or more if needed, plus extra for kneading

1½ teaspoons salt

1 tablespoon caster sugar

1 egg

1 egg yolk

65 g (2½ oz) unsalted butter, softened

oil for greasing

For the topping:

65 g (2½ oz) unsalted butter, softened

150 g (5 oz) caster sugar

grated zest of 1 lemon

Oven temperature:
Gas Mark 8/230°C/450°F

In Vieux Pérouges, a restored medieval village near Lyon, huge cartwheels of bread topped with sugar and lemon emerge from the baker's brick oven at all hours of the day. This smaller version fits a domestic stove.

Sprinkle the yeast over the water and let it stand until dissolved, about 5 minutes. Sift the flour with the salt on to a work surface, add the sugar and make a large well in the centre. Break the egg into the well, add the egg yolk and yeast mixture and mix with your fingertips. Gradually draw in the flour, working the mixture until it forms large crumbs. Press it into a ball; the dough should be soft and slightly sticky but if necessary add more flour.

Flour the work surface and knead the dough by hand for at least 5 minutes until it is smooth and elastic. The dough can also be mixed and kneaded in an electric mixer, using the dough hook. Work in the softened butter and shape the dough into a ball. Put it in an oiled bowl and turn it so the top is also oiled. Cover it with a damp cloth and leave in a warm place to rise until doubled in bulk, 1–1½ hours.

Sprinkle a baking sheet with flour. Knead the dough lightly to knock out the air and roll it out on the baking sheet to the largest round that will fit the sheet. For the topping, spread the softened butter on the dough and sprinkle with sugar and lemon zest. Leave the galette to rise in a warm place for 10–15 minutes. Preheat the oven.

Bake the galette in the oven for 15–20 minutes until the dough is browned and the sugar has melted; cooking time varies with the size of the round. If possible serve it at once while still hot; like all breads, the galette dries when it is kept. It is excellent for breakfast, or served with berries for dessert.

DESSERTS AND LIQUEURS

In France, festive desserts tend to come from the pâtissier, and Burgundy is no exception. The domain of home cooks is puddings, often studded with fruit, and dishes like fritters and pancakes which are so much better cooked at the last moment.

Nowhere are home recipes more valued than in the stillroom where jams, jellies, fruits in liqueur and the liqueurs themselves, are the sign of an accomplished country housewife; I am put to shame by the glowing ranks of jars which seem to be assembled by everyone around me. Now at least I have learned to make clear red currant jelly and to brew a passable glass of cassis, and while doing so I've given more than a fleeting thought to the generations who have done so before me.

LES TARTOUILLATS

Fruit flans in cabbage leaves (Pictured on page 5)   Serves 8

Preparation time: 35 minutes + 35 minutes baking

125 g (4 oz) flour

½ teaspoon salt

250 g (8 oz) caster sugar

4 eggs

250 ml (8 fl oz) milk

butter for greasing

8 large rounded cabbage leaves, with no holes

500 g (1 lb) black cherries or pears

2 tablespoons kirsch

Oven temperature:
Gas Mark 6/200°C/400°F

In the Auxerrois dialect 'tartouiller' means 'to mix well'. In the old days, cabbage leaves served as moulds for this rich custard and fruit mixture, but to avoid leaks I play safe and set the cabbage leaves inside ramekins. In autumn, cherries can be replaced with pears, which are good served with Sauce aux Abricots (Apricot jam sauce, page 79).

For the batter, sift the flour into a bowl with the salt. Stir in the sugar and make a well in the centre. Add the eggs and half the milk and whisk just until the mixture is smooth. Stir in the remaining milk to form a batter. Cover the bowl and leave the batter to stand for about half an hour so the starch grains in the flour swell and thicken it. Preheat the oven.

Bring a large pan of water to boil and blanch the cabbage leaves by boiling them for 2 minutes; then drain them. If the stem ends of the cabbage leaves are large, cut them out. Butter eight ramekins of 175 ml (6 fl oz) capacity and line them with cabbage leaves. Stone the cherries or peel, core and dice the pears. Stir the fruit and kirsch into the batter and spoon the mixture into the cabbage leaves. Trim the edges of the leaves with scissors to leave a generous border above the mould. Set the moulds on a baking sheet and bake them in the oven until the filling is firm and the cabbage leaves are brown, 25–35 minutes. The filling will puff up, but shrink again when it comes out of the oven.

Let the tartouillats cool slightly and then unmould them on to a serving dish or individual plates. Serve them warm or at room temperature. They can be cooked a few hours ahead, but are best eaten on the day of baking.

FRUITS À L'EAU DE VIE

Fruits in brandy   Makes 1.5 litres (2½ pints)

Preparation time: 10 minutes + 2 months storing

125 g (4 oz) caster sugar	*Each year in early summer French supermarkets stock up with forty and sixty per cent alcohol, destined to macerate fruits for the winter. After several months' soaking, the raw spirit acquires a wonderful aroma and when brandy is used, the results are even better. Served in a liqueur glass with one or two of the fruits in the bottom, a tot of this warmly welcomes the casual visitor or nicely rounds off a robust dinner.*
a bottle of brandy	
500 g (1 lb) damsons, apricots, cherries or raspberries	

Stir the sugar into the brandy and leave it for 10–15 minutes until it dissolves. Wash the damsons, apricots and cherries and pick over the raspberries. Leave the stems on the cherries. Prick all the fruit except the raspberries several times with a skewer and pack them in a 1.5-litre (2½-pint) preserving jar. Pour the sugar and brandy over the fruit to cover it completely. Seal the lid and store for at least two months.

Fruits à l'Eau de Vie
Glacé aux Fruits à l'Eau
de Vie ▶

GLACÉ AUX FRUITS À L'EAU DE VIE

Ice cream with fruit in brandy   Serves 10–12

Preparation time: 30 minutes + 15–25 minutes freezing

475 ml (16 fl oz) milk

250 ml (8 fl oz) double cream

7 egg yolks

150 g (5 oz) caster sugar, plus extra if necessary

1.5-litre (2½-pint) jar of fruits à l'eau de vie (fruit in brandy, page 88)

When made into this wickedly rich ice cream, Fruits à l'Eau de Vie (page 88) do double duty, for the brandy is left to drink separately.

To make the custard, first scald the milk with the cream by bringing them just to the boil. Beat the egg yolks with the sugar until they are thick and light and whisk in the hot liquid. Return the mixture to the pan and heat it gently, stirring constantly with a wooden spoon until the custard thickens enough to leave a clear trail when you draw your finger across the back of a spoon. It will curdle if overcooked, so take it at once from the heat and pour it into a cold bowl. Set the bowl over iced water and leave it until the custard is cool, stirring occasionally.

Meanwhile, drain and stone the fruit, reserving the brandy for another occasion. Purée the fruit in a blender or food processor, strain it and measure 750 ml (1¼ pints) of purée.

Stir the fruit purée into the custard and taste, adding more sugar if needed. Freeze the mixture in a churn freezer until set or freeze it in an ordinary freezer for 15–25 minutes. Transfer it to a chilled container and store it in the freezer. Rich ice cream like this keeps well for at least a month.

An hour or two before serving, transfer the ice cream to the refrigerator to soften it slightly. For serving, scoop it into stemmed glasses and, if you like, pour over a little of the fruit brandy.

PAVÉ AUX MARRONS

Chocolate and chestnut paving stone   Serves 8–10

Preparation time: 40 minutes + 24 hours chilling

1 kg (2 lb) fresh chestnuts or canned unsweetened chestnuts

oil for greasing

250 g (8 oz) dessert plain chocolate, chopped

250 ml (8 fl oz) water

175 g (6 oz) unsalted butter

175 g (6 oz) caster sugar

2 tablespoons brandy

For the chantilly cream:

350 ml (12 fl oz) double cream

1–2 tablespoons caster sugar

1 tablespoon brandy

Chocolate has been associated with Lyon from the early seventeenth century, soon after it was brought via Spain from the New World. Since most of France's best chestnuts come from the Ardèche region, just down the Rhône from Lyon, the two are often combined in desserts such as this 'Pavé', shaped like the paving stones which once lined French city streets.

If you are using fresh chestnuts, pierce each nut with the point of a knife. Put them in cold water and bring it to the boil. Drain a few at a time and peel them while they are still hot, removing both outer and inner skins. If they cool and become hard to peel, just reheat them. If you are using canned chestnuts, just drain them; they do not need to be cooked.

Work the chestnuts through a sieve or purée them in a food processor with 2–3 tablespoons of their cooking or canning liquid.

Lightly oil a 7.5 × 10 × 20 cm (3 × 4 × 8-inch) loaf tin, line the base with paper and oil the paper. Melt the chocolate in the water over a low heat and cook, stirring, until it is the consistency of thick cream. Let it cool. Cream the butter and the sugar until they are soft and light. Stir in the cooled chocolate, followed by the chestnut purée and the brandy. Pack the mixture in the prepared tin and cover it with paper. The Pavé should be refrigerated for at least 24 hours and keeps well for up to a week; it can also be frozen.

Not more than 3 hours before serving, unmould the Pavé on to a flat dish or tray, removing the paper. Score the top in a lattice with the point of a knife. Whip the cream until it holds a soft peak, beat in the sugar and brandy and continue whipping until stiff. Fill half into a pastry bag fitted with a medium star tube and decorate the base of the Pavé with a ruff of cream. Serve the remaining cream separately.

SORBET DE RAISINS

Grape sorbet   Serves 6–8

Preparation time: 30 minutes + 15–25 minutes freezing

1 kg (2 lb) black or green grapes

250 g (8 oz) sugar

250 ml (8 fl oz) water

juice of ½ lemon

1 egg white, whisked until frothy

For decoration:

175 g (6 oz) green grapes

175 g (6 oz) black grapes

2 egg whites, whisked until frothy

75 g (3 oz) sugar, or more if needed

As in most wine-growing areas, grapes in Burgundy are destined for the glass and not for the table. If wine grapes are made into sorbet, however, the natural sharpness can be balanced by sugar.

Discard the stems from the 1 kg (2 lb) grapes. Purée the grapes in a food processor or blender, or crush them in a bowl with the end of a rolling pin and then work them through a sieve to extract the juice. It should measure 475 ml (16 fl oz). Heat the sugar with the water until it has dissolved, boil it for 3 minutes and leave it to cool. Stir the lemon juice with sugar syrup to taste into the grape juice; if the grapes are sweet, all the syrup may not be needed.

Freeze the mixture in an ice cream churn or ordinary freezer until it is slushy. Add the egg white and continue churning until firm. Transfer the sorbet to a 1-litre (1⅓-pint) ice cream mould or a chilled bowl, cover and store it in the freezer. It keeps well for a couple of weeks, but after that will start to crystallise.

An hour or two before serving, transfer the sorbet to the refrigerator to soften slightly. Divide the grapes into bunches of two or three. Dip them in beaten egg white and then in sugar and leave them on paper towels to dry. To serve, unmould the sorbet and put the grapes around the edge; alternatively, scoop the sorbet into chilled stemmed glasses and decorate each with a bunch of grapes.

Sorbet de Raisins
Pavé aux Marrons

LIQUEUR DE CASSIS

Blackcurrant liqueur   Makes 2 litres (3½ pints)

Preparation time: 30 minutes + 2–6 months storing

1 kg (2 lb) blackcurrants

1 litre (1¾ pints) vodka or cognac

750 g (1½ lb) caster sugar, or to taste

There are never enough blackcurrants in our garden to satisfy the demand for cassis liqueur, which is easily made at home. A bit rich on its own, a teaspoon of cassis topped up with the local white Aligoté wine makes the excellent summer drink of kir.

Wash the blackcurrants and put them in a 2-litre (3½-pint) preserving jar. Pour over the vodka or cognac, which should just cover the berries. Cover tightly and leave in a cool place at least two months and up to six months.

Put the berries and alcohol in a pan and cook for 10–15 minutes until the juice runs. Work the mixture through a strainer and measure 1.5 litres (2½ pints). Combine the liquid with the sugar in a pan, adding more to taste, and heat gently until the sugar is dissolved. Let the mixture cool and then bottle it and seal it tightly. Cassis liqueur mellows on keeping.

RATAFIA

Grape or apple liqueur   Makes 1.5 litres (2½ pints)

Preparation time: 5 minutes + 6–12 months maturing

1 litre (1¾ pints) fresh-pressed apple or grape juice (page 92)

475 ml (16 fl oz) Calvados apple brandy

As much of a ritual as the presentation by Monsieur Milbert of a bottle of cassis to me at Christmas is the gift to my husband of a bottle of ratafia. Monsieur Milbert makes his with apple juice and his own Calvados, but the more common Burgundian version combines grape juice and brandy.

Mix the apple or grape juice with the brandy. Put in two 750 ml (1¼ pint) bottles and seal them tightly with a cork. Leave in a cool dark place for at least 6 months and a year or more if you like.

INDEX TO RECIPES

Design and layout: Ken Vail Graphic Design
Photography: Laurie Evans
Food preparation for photography: Pete Smith
Stylist: Alison Williams
Illustrations: Mandy Doyle
Text and recipe editor: Denise Cassis
Typesetting: Westholme Graphics